THE JOCKEY CLUB'S

·

ILLUSTRATED HISTORY OF

THOROUGHBRED RACING

·

IN AMERICA

Helenus   Jerry

THE JOCKEY CLUB'S
ILLUSTRATED HISTORY OF
THOROUGHBRED RACING
IN AMERICA

TEXT BY EDWARD L. BOWEN

A BULFINCH PRESS BOOK

LITTLE, BROWN AND COMPANY

BOSTON • NEW YORK • TORONTO • LONDON

First Edition

ISBN 0-8212-2059-4

Library of Congress Cataloging-in-Publication information is available.

Bulfinch Press is an imprint and trademark of
Little, Brown and Company (Inc.). Published simultaneously in Canada by
Little, Brown and Company (Canada) Limited.

*The Jockey Club's Illustrated History of
Thoroughbred Racing in America*
was created and produced by Navarre Media, Inc.

CREATOR AND EDITOR-IN-CHIEF: Carl Navarre
DESIGNER: J.C. Suarès
PICTURE EDITOR: Peter C. Jones
ASSITANT TO THE EDITOR: Marybeth MacFarland
ASSISTANT PICTURE EDITOR: Lisa MacDonald
ASSISTANT DESIGNER: Tyrone Randall
TEXT COORDINATORS: Jane Martin, Peter Lewis
PRODUCTION: Thomasson-Grant, Charlottesville, Virginia

PRINTED IN SINGAPORE

PAGES 2–3
Illustrative of the genre of sporting art spawned by Thoroughbred racing in England,
J. F. Herring, Sr. depicts the final furlongs of the 1826 Doncaster Cup won by Fleur de
Lis over Mulatto. Courtesy Paul Mellon Collection.

PAGES 4–5
A champion of the 1890s and later a profound influence on the breed,
Domino is shown winning the 1893 Matron Stakes as depicted by Gean Smith.
Courtesy Mrs. Walter M. Jeffords, Jr.

PAGES 6–7
The fortuitously named Upset administered Man o' War his only defeat, stunning
the great horse in the 1919 Sanford Stakes in Saratoga. Photograph by C. C. Cook.
Courtesy Keeneland-Cook Collection.

PAGES 8–9
The feel of the Turf fascinates photographers as well as painters and sculptors.
Photograph by Dell Hancock.

PAGE 10
Citation, Triple Crown winner of 1948 and the first equine millionaire, is shown
with the great jockey Eddie Arcaro aboard. Courtesy Culver Pictures.

PAGE 14
Poised for action. Photograph by Dell Hancock.

TABLE OF CONTENTS

THE JOCKEY CLUB'S

·

ILLUSTRATED HISTORY OF

THOROUGHBRED RACING

·

IN AMERICA

STEVEN CRIST

As the nineties began, American Thoroughbred racing was facing numerous crises. Racehorse owners could not afford to run for the small purses being offered. Tracks were presenting far too many racing dates in competition with one another. A lack of uniform rules from state to state made regulation an elusive goal. Amid these grave issues, those who cared deeply about racing and horses were calling for the creation of a new body, or perhaps a national czar, to supervise the teetering sport.

Whoever writes the introduction to The Jockey Club's book in the year 2094, celebrating its first two centuries, is welcome to recycle the preceding

TO THE LEFT
Riders and assistant starters wait for the last horses to be loaded into the gate prior to a race at Santa Anita. Photograph by Norman Mauskopf.

paragraph. Every word of it applies as much to the 1890s as it does to the 1990s, and it is 3-to-5 on the morning line that it will be just as valid in the good old 2090s as well.

Thoroughbred racing will outlive all of us, most of its fellow sports, and perhaps even some of these problems. It is bigger and stronger than all of them. Distilled to its essence, racing is at every level about the pursuit of quality and a striving for excellence. The notion of improving the breed permeates every aspect of the sport. We run races to entertain but also to inform, to find the horses who will produce a better horse a generation from now.

By definition, then, Thoroughbred racing is always moving forward on a line between here and perfection. Occasionally we get a glimpse of the goal, Secretariat or Personal Ensign, and we wait and hunger for another.

All games need rules, and racing works best when those who care about its quality and fairness devise its structure. The chaos of the sport in the 1890s led men who cherished racing to form The Jockey Club in 1894.

It has prospered its first century amid numerous changes of activity but no wavering of purpose. While many functions of supervising and operating racing have been subsumed by government, which protects its own and the public's interest in varying degrees, The Jockey Club has adapted to the changing world around a sport that in essence changes little.

Maintaining the integrity of the Thoroughbred breed by registering the foals born every year remains the heart of the operation, while newer activities such as collecting and distributing racing and breeding information will benefit racing's loyal fans, who bankroll the sport but whose interests too often run last. Other worthy endeavors include continuing research into the ailments that afflict the ever-fragile Thoroughbred, and the training and accreditation of racing officials.

While the problems of racing may be as old as the game itself, the years ahead may legitimately be the most trying. Over the last century, the horse has vanished from

TO THE RIGHT

Santa Anita is known for its California sun, but even there downpours can change the track to sloppy. Photograph by Norman Mauskopf.

all other avenues of American life, weakening a bond that was at the core of the sport's appeal. More ominously, after decades of enjoying a monopoly on legalized gambling in most of the country, racing now is competing with inferior but flashier wagers, and it seems only a matter of time before casinos and ballgame bookmakers are franchised throughout the land.

To survive, racing will have to adapt its product to changing public tastes without compromising the ingredients of its greatness. The public's betting money is the lifeblood of the industry, and racing will have to compete for that money far more effectively than it has in these early years of competition. Yet the sport must never lose the integrity and mission of quality that have sustained it, lest those who are attracted to it find it a hollow pursuit.

There are always signs that racing is responding to these challenges, though each response has its price.

The Breeders' Cup has given national focus to the racing calendar and given the sport a new window of exposure at season's end, but has diminished the importance of other races, such as The Jockey Club Gold Cup at Belmont Park.

Offtrack betting is becoming more widely available, and while it will lead to higher overall wagering levels, track attendance will continue to decline.

Simulcasting races among tracks has captured the public fancy and brought better racing to many patrons, but a need for less live racing will eventually shutter some smaller tracks and reduce the demand for horses from the breeding industry.

All these developments can be absorbed. They are nothing next to the simple greatness of racing: My horse is faster than your horse, and I'll prove it down at the meadow. There will always be Thoroughbreds to carry the blood of these age-old challenges, and people who love them watching from the stands.

TO THE LEFT
Belmont Stakes Day brings large crowds to Belmont Park on Long Island, whatever the weather. Photograph by Norman Mauskopf.

FOUNDATIONS OF THE TURF

The President of the United States was determined to return to some semblance of his earlier days as a racehorse owner. With a brazen streak inherent in his public persona, he brought several racehorses to the stables of the White House, but he was not unmindful about public sentiment. He raced them in the name of A. J. Donelson, although they were widely known to be owned by the President himself.

Andrew Jackson had been assailed in the political campaign of 1824 as a "horse-racer, gambler, and brawler." If this combination were not quite what the young nation was looking for in its leader in 1824, neither did it disqualify

AT LEFT

The Epsom Derby is more than 200 years old and remains the centerpeice of racing in its founding land of England. Top-hatted aristocrats share Epsom Downs on Derby Day with gypsies and commoners. Here an Epsom scene from the 1830s is depicted by James Pollard. Courtesy Paul Mellon Collection.

23

a fellow for life. He was duly elected in 1828.

Thus did President Jackson illustrate one of the paradoxes of the sport of racing. On the one hand, it has the image of the highest social order, replete with aristocrats—both of genetic and professional ascendency to that designation. On the other hand, because gambling is one dimension of the sport, the turf is seen by some as the habitat of a lower, and corrupt, element.

In his place and time, horsemanship was as routine in life as driving an automobile is today. Born in 1767, Jackson at thirteen was a mounted orderly for the cavalry during the War of Revolution, and as a grown soldier he commanded the winning effort in the Battle of New Orleans during the War of 1812. In between, he had been an Indian fighter, teacher, saddler's apprentice, and a graduate of law studies in North Carolina. He also frolicked through an inheritance of $1,600 that fell into his lap at the age of

sixteen. The lure of racing was strong in Andrew Jackson. When he decided to settle in Natchez, Mississippi, he intended to lay out a racecourse on a piece of property that seemed perfectly suited for it. Instead, he eventually settled in Nashville, where he was one of the club of fellows who established a racecourse at Clover Bottom in 1800. There his horse Truxton defeated Ploughboy in a match race that drew what Jackson once called the "largest concourse of people I ever saw assembled, unless as an army." Indirectly connected to Truxton's victory over Ploughboy was the duel in which Old Hickory took a round in the chest, but stood firmly long enough to deliver his opponent into the next world.

Truxton later stood at stud for $20, or $30 to insure, to be paid in "merchantable ginned cotton"—a bargain providing a tiny insight into life in America at the time. In one of Truxton's matches, against Greyhound, the

ABOVE
Andrew Jackson was such an ardent sportsman that he stabled his racehorse on the White House grounds during his presidency. As a bow to ambiguous public opinion, he raced them in the name of his private secretary, A. J. Donelson. Painting by John Wood Dodge. Courtesy *The Blood-Horse*.

AT RIGHT
The artist Henri de Lattre was among many who benefitted by the sentiment and pride the landed gentry left for their horses and dogs. Indeed, it was often said that a sportsman would pay more for a portrait of his horses than for one of his wife. Courtesy Mrs. Walter M. Jeffords, Jr.

$5,000 a side included $1,500 worth of apparel. Truxton's victory, wrote historian John Hervey, left Jackson "eased in his finances and replenished in his wardrobe." The winning owner thereupon purchased the defeated Greyhound. Much of Jackson's energies on the racecourse involved trying to defeat Jesse Haynie's mare Maria. For several seasons, Jackson sought to purchase a horse that could lower Maria's colors, at one point negotiating with William R. Johnson, known as the Napoleon of the Turf, to purchase Pacolet "without regard to price." He never succeeded, and late in life when asked if he had ever taken up any cause and failed, Jackson was said to reply, "Nothing that I can remember, except Haynie's Maria. I could not beat her."

President Jackson's vaunted Truxton and his exasperating rival, Maria, both had been sired by Diomed. The importation of an Epsom Derby winner to sire champions in this country was to be a relatively frequent pattern over the centuries. England spawned the Thoroughbred, and in many ways the American colonists and their successors, American citizens, imitated matters English despite the feelings of hostility that flared from time to time with the occasional war.

Horse racing's origins are in antiquity, and there is evidence of it being staged on English soil during the Roman occupation. There was also racing held at the Smithfield horse market in London during the reign of Henry II. In general, however, wrote the English turf historian Roger Mortimer, "development of horse racing in England can really be said to date from the 17th Century."

During the reign of James I, racing took on aspects of an organized sport. James visited Newmarket for the first time in 1605. He lodged at first at an inn called the Griffin, but was so taken by the area that he made enough return visits to justify—in his mind—building a royal palace there. According to Mortimer in *The Jockey*

AT RIGHT

Priam won the 1830 Epsom Derby amid ironic circumstances. He was owned and trained by Bill Chifney, whose father, Sam Chifney, had been wrongly accused of chicanery when riding for the Prince of Wales in 1791. The prince, later George IV, gave up racing for a time in protest, but had returned and owned a runner which was beaten by Priam at Epsom. Painting by John Ferneley. Courtesy National Museum of Racing.

Club, "James's affection for Newmarket was based largely on his enthusiasm for hawking and hunting, and his interest in horses lay chiefly in the fact that they enabled him to follow hounds." Nevertheless, some of his Scottish courtiers, accustomed to racing in the north, must have taken one look at the vast, relatively level Newmarket Heath and concluded immediately what God had intended to take place there.

James I recognized the value of racing as a catalyst for improving England's equine stock, but busied himself with his other pursuits. On the bizarre advice of his royal physician, he would thrust his arms and legs into the entrails of the deer kills in his hunting expeditions. There is no account that traipsing along after James I following one of these charming ceremonies became known as the Spoor of Kings. Nevertheless, the phrase sport of kings over time was usurped from hunting-to-hounds and affixed to racing. Charles I fed this with his own love of the turf.

Oliver Cromwell was not personally opposed to the sport. Its repression during the Commonwealth was prompted by Cromwell's discomfort over any event that tended to bring together a large number of Royalists to grumble amongst themselves. Cromwell did, however, maintain a stud, the remnants of which became the nucleus of Charles II's Royal Stud, after the Restoration. Charles II was so enthusiastic over horse racing that he personally rode in matches. As the amount of betting increased, Charles II decreed himself the supreme steward at Newmarket. This was around 1665, by which time Governor Richard Nicolls, in New York across the Atlantic, gave the name New Market to the course he laid out on Long Island.

During the time of King William III, the royal trainer was one Tregonwell Frampton. Mortimer wrote that in some quarters it was regarded that "sin came upon the Turf with the advent of Frampton." Nevertheless, it was Frampton who recognized that the activity had grown to such proportions that it needed some order and rules. By the time of his death in 1727, he was known as the Father of the Turf. His earlier critics might therefore have considered the turf as a bastard. Be that as it may, Frampton to this day, is revered for his pioneering role in the evolution that led eventually to formation of England's Jockey Club and formalization of racing rules and record keeping.

By 1740, racing had become so popular that there seemed a danger of too many small courses being established. Fearing that such gyp circuits would breed chicanery, Parliament passed legislation setting limits on the amount of racing. Some 150 years later, similar concerns were in part responsible for the formation of The Jockey Club in this country, although no federal acts were involved.

The seventeenth century saw not only the seeds of formalization of the turf, but also the primitive foundations of the Thoroughbred breed. During the late seven-

ABOVE
Edward Troye was one of America's most important nineteenth-century equine artists.
He portrayed Arabian horses as well as American Thoroughbreds. Courtesy National Museum of Racing.

ON PAGE 30
Wagner was among many distinguished runners depicted by Edward Troye. Courtesy National Museum of Racing.

teenth century and early eighteenth century, three key horses were among the many Oriental stallions imported into England. These were the Beyerly Turk (probably from Turkey, 1690), the Darley Arabian (from Asia Minor, 1704), and the Godolphin Arabian (via France, about 1730). Although there were earlier foundation stallions, these three became the wellhead to which all later Thoroughbreds would trace. Each of them fathered a sire line that would be identified by a descendant, and so the lines of Eclipse, Matchem, and Herod likewise became prominent in the ancestry of all modern Thoroughbreds. Eclipse, the greatest of the three influences by the present day, was foaled in 1764. He was undefeated on the turf, and his blood became pervasive throughout the world.

In 1730, Bulle Rock became the first stallion imported to the colonies that was identifiable at least loosely as a "Thoroughbred." He was a son of the Darley Arabian, as was England's Flying Childers, regarded as

the first "wonder horse" among a sequence of milestone shapers of the sport and breed. Bulle Rock was an accomplished racer, but had not been a noted stud horse at the time of his arrival in Virginia in 1730. He was twenty-one years old then, but as he was representative of the burgeoning breed in the motherland, his issue were widely sought.

It was the arrival near the end of that century of another twenty-one-year-old stallion that had a focusing effect on the Thoroughbred of this country. In 1798, John Hoomes of Bowling Green in Virginia, had an agent at large in England, and he purchased Diomed for fifty guineas. Diomed's seller, Sir Charles Bunbury, must have thought he had put one over on the bumpkin colonists in the backward New World. Diomed at one time had been regarded the best racehorse since Eclipse himself, but by the time Hoomes bought him, he was described as "a tried and proved bad foal getter."

Nevertheless, Diomed was already assured a distin-

PAGE 31
Eastern stallions were instrumental in the establishment of the Thoroughbred, being crossed with various European strains. Painting by Edward Troye.
Courtesy Mrs. Walter M. Jeffords, Jr.

AT LEFT
Three views of Dexter. Painting by Edward Troye. Courtesy Mrs. Walter M. Jeffords, Jr.

guished place in English racing history, for in 1780 he won the first running of the Derby Stakes at Epsom. The advent of that noble race dated from a rowdyish evening at Lord Derby's country house, the Oakes, near the frequently visited spa town of Epsom. When the swells at the party decided to plan a race for three-year-old fillies the following spring, they named it the Oakes, in honor of their host's home. (It has become known without the letter e, as the Oaks.) The follow-up of that race was one for three-year-old colts, to be run a year later, in 1780. Legend has it that a coin toss decided whether it, too, would be named in honor of the host, Lord Derby, or Sir Charles Bunbury, a guest that evening and the most prominent personage on the turf at the time. At any rate, the following year was staged the first running of the Derby, destined to become an element in the very marrow of the sport. Sir Charles Bunbury may have lost the coin toss, but he won the prize, sending out Diomed as his representative.

(Readily understandable is the repeated sentiment that the Muses were smiling on that coin. Had the result been otherwise, the question can be asked, would the new Epsom event have caught on as the Bunbury Stakes? Would jockey clubs around the world have emulated it, creating the Kentucky Bunbury instead of the Kentucky Derby, the American Bunbury, the Santa Anita Bunbury? While we might be amused at the thought, testimony of no less than Oscar Wilde suggests that the word Bunbury can be, in fact, rather versatile. In *The Importance of Being Earnest*, Wilde's character Algernon explains that he has often ducked out of unpromising social engagements by pleading the need to visit his invalid friend, Bunbury, whose being and name are both his inventions. Algernon boasts that "I have 'Bunburyed' all over Shropshire . . ." He declares his term "Bunburyist" an "incomparable expression.")

Given the support of monarchs, and races such as the Derby, horse racing pumped on within the heart of

AT RIGHT
American Eclipse was unbeaten on American racecourses from 1818 to 1823. He was named in honor of the pivotal English stallion Eclipse, his great-great-grandsire.
Painting by Edward Troye. Courtesy National Museum of Racing.

THE CELEBRATED HORSE

SIR ARCHIE,

WILL STAND THE ENSUING SEASON

At my Stable in Northampton County, North-Carolina, about three miles from the Court-House, nine miles from the town of Halifax, and twenty-one miles from Belfiel'l, Virginia.

He will Cover Mares at Fifty Dollars the Season, payable on the first of January next, or Forty-Five Dollars if paid within the Season, (with one dollar to the Groom in all cases.)

Such of Archie's Friends, that lives at a distance, will send their Notes with the Mares, payable on the first of January next—Also, feeding of the Mares to be paid when taken away.

The season will commence the first of February next, and terminate the Fifteenth of July.—Extensive fields of Small Grain and Clover are sowed for the benefit of the Mares, (which may be left with the Horse) with the addition of grain feeding, at 25 cents per day.—Separate enclosures are provided for Mares with Colts.—No pains will be spared in taking the best possible care of Mares, &c. which may be left, but no responsibility for escapes or accidents.

SIR ARCHIE'S BLOOD, GREAT SIZE....Performance on the Turf, and celebrity as a Foal getter, are sufficient recommendations. WILLIAM AMIS.

January 1, 1817   Compiler Press.—Halifax, N. C.

England. Subsequent monarchs were not always supporters, but aside from a few eras of rampant chicanery, the turf seemed to speak to the souls of more Englishmen than its gambling aspect offended. Classic winners were bred in the name of the Royal Studs during Queen Victoria's time, although she and the straightlaced Prince Consort were not active and Victoria frowned upon the sporting life pursued by her heir, the Prince of Wales (Edward VII). Nevertheless, Edward's patronage of racing encouraged the sport and helped it through a shaky period. Other twentieth-century monarchs have continued the Royal Studs and stables, and none has been so keen—nor as knowledgeable—as the present Queen, Elizabeth II.

The turf's role in English life and thought was eloquently described by the great jockey Sir Gordon Richards, who won the Epsom Derby on Pinza in 1953, defeating the young Queen Elizabeth's Aureole. Said Sir Gordon: "Racing is in the character of the people of this country. It's like the sea. There's something about the sea in the minds of kids living in the heart of London who've never seen it. And there's something of racing in the British character . . . As far as I'm concerned, racing is a form of public life."

In the time of Diomed, this chromosomal involvement perhaps was not yet established. Not even a Derby winner enjoyed the status that he would in later eras, but despite his age and diminished rank, Diomed arrived on these shores in time to shore up the standing

AT RIGHT

Many horses, both racehorse and revered riding mounts, have been named for personalities. One of them, Archy, was painted by Henry de Lattre. (Courtesy Mrs. Walter M. Jeffords, Jr.)
Another Archy was the great early American sire Sir Archy. He was first named Robert Burns, but then was renamed in honor of one of his original owners, Captain Archibald Randolph.

Mr. DeLattre.

Marchy

1830

of the American racehorse. Moreover, Colonel Hoomes made a deal that might have left Sir Charles Bunbury wondering just who was the bumpkin. Hoomes penned glowing reports of the horse, such as a letter to Colonel John Tayloe III—"I wish you could see Diomed. I think him the finest horse I ever saw . . . He is near 16 hands and much admired by everyone who sees him." The following year, Hoomes turned his fifty-guinea oldster over to Thomas Goode and Miles Selden for the price of 1,000 pounds sterling!

Diomed lived on to the age of thirty-one. In addition to President Jackson's Truxton and Haynie's Maria, he begot about a dozen other distinguished American runners. The greatest, and most influential of them, was Sir Archy. Foaled in 1805, Sir Archy was bred by Colonel Tayloe and Captain Archibald Randolph, and was purchased by Colonel Johnson for $1,500 despite indifferent early form. Colonel Johnson, the "Napoleon," had won sixty-one matches of sixty-three entered by his horses over a two-year period, and his judgment was upheld again in the case of Sir Archy. While the tradition in American racing had been for the training and riding of horses to be turned over to specialist slaves, Colonel Johnson employed an Englishman, Arthur Taylor, to train his horses. Taylor was based in Warrenton, North Carolina, and sent Sir Archy back into action as a budding champion. He won 4 of his 5 races at four in 1809. In the stud, he was so dominant that he created an inbreeding problem in the burgeoning breeding and racing industry of the new nation. He had nearly 100 sons advertised at stud at one time or another, and 160 of his daughters became producers. He became frequently described as "the Godolphin Arabian of America."

Sir Archy's sons included Timoleon, sire of the great horse Boston. In turn, Boston sired Lexington, a champion that rampaged through American racing before the Civil War, and whose blood shaped the following era.

AT RIGHT
One of the great events of antebellum racing was the rematch of Boston and the mare Fashion at the Union Course in 1842. Fashion repeated her earlier triumph before a crowd said to number 50,000. Painting by John A. Woodside. Courtesy Mrs. Walter M. Jeffords, Jr.

Lexington, by Boston and out of Alice Carneal, was bred by Dr. Elisha Warfield, who was the most important Kentucky horseman in his day and would be looked back upon as Father of the Kentucky Turf. A foal of 1850, Lexington was secured later by Richard Ten Broeck, one of the first international sportsmen. Ten Broeck was the primary shareholder in the flourishing Metairie Course in New Orleans, and much later he sent Parole abroad to win England's City and Suburban Handicap—the first instance of an American-bred horse winning a major event in the Motherland.

The impulse that English horses were to be sought for the betterment at home, however, was still strong. When R. A. Alexander, owner of the 2,000-acre Woodburn Stud in Kentucky, was in England in the middle 1850s, he was looking for a young English stallion prospect. By chance, he ran into fellow American Ten Broeck, who convinced him that he need not have looked farther than his own Bluegrass neighborhood.

Ten Broeck sold him the young Lexington, winner of six of his seven races and then starting his career at stud. The price was $15,000, and Alexander declared in the face of bemusement that he would someday sell a son of Lexington for a greater price. He made good on his vow, selling Norfolk for $15,001—whatever that might have equaled in "ginned cotton."

Lexington led the American sire list sixteen times, a feat unmatched. Even England's immortal St. Simon led the sire list abroad only nine times (between 1890–1901). Lexington would have been even more successful but for the outbreak of the Civil War. The war harmed his record in two ways: Racing was virtually brought to a standstill, especially in the South, and a large number of his foals from several crops were hastily requisitioned by raiding parties from both Union and Confederate armies.

Great wars tend to leave behind worlds massively changed. In the case of the Civil War, horse racing as it had been known was an image of the past once the maelstrom subsided. "The flames and fury of the Civil War produced the funeral pyre of racing as America had known it hitherto," wrote John Hervey in *Racing In America*. Not all change was due to the war itself, however. For example, Thoroughbred racing for much of the earlier days had been conducted in heats, up to four miles for each of three contests in a single day. The fashion of the extreme stayer already was waning, Hervey found. In 1837, there were recorded 62 races at four-mile heats and 247 as short as one-mile heats. By 1860, there were only 24 races at four-mile heats, 313 at one-mile, and others in between.

Hervey felt that Lexington's blood was the one element which was both a prewar and a postwar force.

Whatever the preferred distance, the sons and daughters of the great Woodburn stallion prevailed. Racing was established at Saratoga in 1863, despite the ongoing war, and nine of the early runnings of its enduring Travers Stakes were won by offspring of Lexington.

When the nation's oldest Derby, the Jersey Derby, was first run, in 1864, the winner was the unbeaten Norfolk, Lexington's $15,001 son; the runner-up was Lexington's son, Kentucky, suffering his only defeat in a career of twenty-two races. In the same crop came Asteroid, the undefeated midwestern racer.

Woodburn Stud had inaugurated an annual yearling sale in 1857, based on the practice of a few major English breeders who sold a number of their

ABOVE

Boston was in such poor condition at seventeen, that he was supported by a special hammock in his stall. Despite his condition, that spring he sired the two great champions, Lexington and Lecomte. Painting by Henri de Lattre. Courtesy Mrs. Walter M. Jeffords, Jr.

ON FOLLOWING PAGE

Lexington was America's leading sire sixteen times. His record would have been even greater but for Union and Confederate troops' tendency to confiscate his issue for more bellicose purposes than racing. Painting by Edward Troye. Courtesy National Museum of Racing.

yearlings annually. The sales were interrupted by the war, but then resumed. They continued until 1893, the time of a great financial depression, when the sad conclusion was reached to disperse the farm.

For some 200 years, racing in this country had been an important adjunct to an agrarian society. In the Colonial period, there were eight major courses in Virginia, six in Maryland, and four in South Carolina, as recorded by Hervey, while in the North there was racing in New Jersey, Pennsylvania, and Massachusetts, as well as New York. In some fifty years after the Revolution, growth was more evident in the South, where major racing developed also in North Carolina, Georgia, Kentucky, Tennessee, Florida, Alabama, Mississippi, and Louisiana. Also during that era, it spread into the Midwest. Arkansas (Oaklawn Park at Hot Springs has been one of the most resurgent tracks in the latter 1900s) had racing then, as did Illinois, Ohio, Indiana, Wisconsin, Minnesota, Iowa, Michigan, and

Missouri. The sport also had reached California. The Civil War saw only sporadic meetings, and in many of these states there was no revival.

Another change in the conduct of racing from the eras of Sir Archy and Boston was that match races were being replaced by club races, events open to horses owned by members of the various organized jockey clubs. The desire to see the entire race and not be subject to out-of-view chicanery brought the mile oval, or circular track, into vogue, and American racing gradually switched to dirt, or "skinned" tracks, instead of the all-encompassing grass courses of England. (This practice was initiated with New York's Union Course in 1821.)

With club racing, the sport became almost wholly democratized, both as to participants and spectators. Hervey swept across the ages succinctly: "What had begun as a semi-private, semi-amateur sport which the public was allowed to witness as a concession by those who pursued it, had evolved into a great popular amuse-

ON PAGE 43

Ruthless, a filly, won the first running of the Belmont Stakes, in 1867. Painting by Edward Troye. Courtesy Mrs. Walter M. Jeffords, Jr.

AT LEFT

Asteroid was among many champions sired by Lexington. He is shown with groom Old Ance and trainer Ed Brown, known as Brown Dick. Painting by Edward Troye. Courtesy Mrs. Walter M. Jeffords, Jr.

ment for the whole of the citizenry, conducted as a rule by associations semi-professional if not wholly professional in character."

Professionalism also had begun to shape the breeding industry, even before the Civil War. By Hervey's reckoning, the emergence of Kentucky as the breeding center (surpassing Tennessee, Maryland, and Virginia) was in large measure authored because the Bluegrass breeders organized themselves on a professional basis. It was after the Civil War that absentee landlords became major landowners, leaving the agricultural work to employed farm managers.

The concept of the racetrack as a massive, luxurious, and stabilized ocean liner was given impetus soon after the war. Leonard Jerome envisioned a jockey club similar to that which conducted racing in Newmarket in England. He wanted this situated as a suburb of America's great metropolis, New York City, and he purchased the old Bathgate estate in 1865. By the next year,

he opened Jerome Park, an edifice with spacious dining rooms, a bandstand, a gallery lined with portraits of famous racehorses—both English and American—and a grand ballroom. The American Jockey Club had 50 life members and 1,250 subscribing members, and club balls were frequently held after the races. Jerome, whose daughter Jenny was Winston Churchill's mother, also was involved with the Coney Island Jockey Club, which built the racetrack at Sheepshead Bay, and with John A. Morris's grand Morris Park.

August Belmont I was president of the American Jockey Club, which owned Jerome Park, and the first Belmont Stakes was run there in 1867. It was won by the filly Ruthless, owned by John A. Morris, whose scarlet silks were the oldest in America by the time a latter-day John A. Morris (a great-grandson) won the Coaching Club American Oaks with Missile Belle in 1970.

Ruthless was ridden in the Belmont by jockey Gilpatrick, who bridged some eras in his own right. As

AT LEFT

As a holdover from the days when slaves were assigned to ride their owner's racehorses, black jockeys were prominent through the late nineteenth and early twentieth centuries. The stylish Isaac Murphy, rider of three Kentucky Derby winners, is shown at a Salvator Club clambake in 1890. Photograph courtesy Keeneland Library.

Gilbert Patrick, he had ridden the celebrated Boston when he was beaten by the mare Fashion in four-mile heats before a crowd said to exceed 50,000 at the Union Course twenty-five years earlier. Gilpatrick also rode Lexington. The gentlemanly jockey was regarded as the best rider in America.

The revival of racing also spread south and west. In 1868, the governor of Maryland, horseman Oden Bowie, promised during a dinner party at Saratoga that Maryland would have a track ready in two years if a new race being organized were to be assigned there. Thus, Pimlico opened in 1870 with the Dinner Party Stakes, later known as the Dixie Handicap and still being run annually. Its first winner was Preakness, which lent his name to a classic in the state where colonists had launched some of the earliest racing in America.

In 1875, Colonel Merriwether Lewis Clark launched his Kentucky Jockey Club track in Louisville, Kentucky (Churchill Downs), with the Kentucky Derby as part of a series imitating the English classic structure (Two Thousand Guineas, One Thousand Guineas, Derby, Oaks, and St. Leger Stakes). Only the Derby caught on and survived as a national classic. The first Derby winner, Aristides, was ridden by the black rider Oliver Lewis. As a holdover from slavery days, when individuals were assigned as jockeys, black riders were prominent through several decades after the Civil War, on into the twentieth century. The great black jockey Isaac Murphy won the Kentucky Derby three times in the 1880s and 1890s, and Jimmy Winkfield won consecutive Derbys in 1901 and 1902.

Racing also was revived after the Civil War in Louisiana, but many of the southern states (including Virginia and the Carolinas) important in the antebellum turf remained silent. As Hervey lamented of the likes of Richmond, Charleston, and Savannah, "never again were the golden glories to be renewed."

By 1894, as the great vise of depression tightened

AT RIGHT
Among the many tracks that flourished for a time but disappeared was the Bennings Race Track near Washington, D.C., circa 1890. Photograph by C. C. Cook.
Courtesy George S. Bolster Collection of the Historical Society of Saratoga Springs.

and then released its grip, horse racing in America had again become a national sport. While the Civil War had ended "golden glories" in many places, racetracks sprang up again from coast to coast. The turf had proven resilient. Racing's shape was far different from its appearance at the dawn of the nineteenth century, but the sport was one ingredient in the pungence of America emergent. Now, another century was at hand.

AT RIGHT

Hanover won fourteen important races within twelve weeks at three in 1887. He later became a leading sire. Painting by C. L. Zellinsky. Courtesy National Museum of Racing.

THE GREAT CHAMPIONS

A great racehorse is a gift to the sporting world. Like a Picasso painting, the Thoroughbred might seem nothing more than an inscrutable, somewhat superfluous creation to much of the general public. Yet to those who sense a connection with the horse, it is a being of both grace and fire, both beauty and power. Like a Picasso, a Thoroughbred embodies an eddy of life forces— pulse and passion, at once lovely in its fineness and engulfing in its energies.

The champion racehorse can elicit verbal and visceral tribute, even from those whose fortunes are tied to rival competitors. When Commander J. K. L.

AT LEFT

In an age when other sports had Babe Ruth, Jack Dempsey, and Red Grange, racing had a Big Red of its own — Man o' War. Beaten but once on the racetrack, he remained such a public idol as a stallion, that his funeral was broadcast nationally on radio. Painting by Martin Stainforth. Courtesy Mrs. Walter M. Jeffords, Jr.

Ross watched Man o' War glide to the wire in the last race of the horse's career, he could only mutter, "What a marvel!" As recalled years later by his son, Ross was moved to such heartfelt tribute by the majesty of the first of two bright chestnut racehorses that charged through the dusty stretch at Kenilworth Park in Windsor, Ontario, in 1919. While the horse that arrested the Canadian industrialist and sportsman was known to the sporting world as Man o' War, to Ross he bore the name of Nemesis. It was, after all, Ross's own champion Sir Barton that was left seven lengths behind as Man o' War—the Big Red of sport's Golden Age—strode home through the slanting autumn sunlight.

Ross' involuntary expression of sportsmanship is not unique. Many years later, the distinguished publisher and sportsman John Hay (Jock) Whitney gazed at the latest champion, Alfred G. Vanderbilt's "Gray Ghost," Native Dancer. Whitney and his sister were sending out Straight Face to meet Native Dancer in the 1954 Metropolitan Handicap. With a chance at a victory of his own, Whitney instead mused, "It's strange, but I hope the Dancer wins."

American racing in the last century frequently has been visited by such noble equine creatures. Sometimes a great champion stands alone, a Citation or Secretariat, supreme upon the stage. At other times, champions are sent to match strides with one another, and thus we have the rivalries of Affirmed versus Alydar, or Whirlaway and Alsab.

The aforementioned Man o' War still ranks in horsemen's lore

ABOVE

Man o' War was allowed to drink, literally, from the cup of triumph by owner Samuel D. Riddle (right) and trainer Louis Feustel.

Courtesy National Museum of Racing.

and history as one of the greatest. He was the fulfillment of the American stewardship of the bloodlines that had their haphazard beginnings in England. Man o' War epitomized the horsemen's credo for judging greatness: "It isn't just what he did; it's how he did it."

In Man o' War's case, the "what" and the "how" were both spectacular. The high-headed chestnut colt won 20 of 21 races at two and three, in 1919 and 1920. His earnings of $249,465 were a record at the time. His only loss came at two, when he was buffeted by traffic in Saratoga's Sanford Stakes. He failed to come to terms with a colt that had been named as if in prophecy of an historic distinction; the only horse ever to beat Man o' War was named Upset.

The Sanford loss was a reminder that all horses, even Man o' War, are flesh and blood and subject to the whims of turfdom's fates, but the reminder faded with the months. At three years old, Man o' War won all of his eleven races, eight of them in record times either for the track or all of American racing.

Retired to stud at Faraway Farm in Kentucky, he became more than a famous racehorse. He was a tourist attraction and the embodiment of the yearning for greatness that resides in the souls of mankind. He was depicted in a heroic statue by Herbert Haseltine and forever anointed "the mostess hoss" by his groom, Will Harbut.

As a great American racehorse Man o' War had been preceded by the likes of Hanover, Salvator, Domino, Sysonby, and Colin. The champions that followed included the best of his own offspring, War Admiral.

Man o' War never raced in America's signature event, the Kentucky Derby. Samuel Riddle, who had

ABOVE

Samuel D. Riddle clung to Man o' War, turning down princely offers. He has purchased the horse as a yearling for $5,000, outbidding Robert L. Gerry, who was said to be looking for a hunter prospect. Photograph by Brownie Leach. Courtesy *The Blood-Horse*.

purchased him as a yearling for $5,000 because his breeder, August Belmont II, had gone off to war, believed the 1 1/4 miles of the springtime Derby too much for a three year old. By War Admiral's time, however, the Derby's connection to two other spring races had become so cemented as to increase even its own prestige: the Preakness Stakes in Baltimore, Maryland, and the Belmont Stakes in New York. Collectively, they became known as the Triple Crown and stood as the pinnacle among achievements and challenges. Sir Barton, Man o' War's old foil, had been the first to sweep all three, and by the time Gallant Fox (1930) and his son Omaha (1935) had followed suit, the Triple Crown was established as a unit.

Riddle, then, was prevailed upon to allow War Admiral to take his chance in the Derby, and Big Red's little brown son duly began his own sweep of the Triple Crown. He was followed in the next dozen years by Triple Crown winners Whirlaway (1941), Count Fleet (1943), Assault (1946), and Citation (1948). Citation was the first horse to challenge seriously Man o' War's reputation as the best of the century. Man o' War and Citation, although comparable in qualities, were of different styles. The late Joe Palmer, one of the sport's acclaimed writers, saw in Man o' War something akin to "a living flame," while Citation was "a well-oiled machine." Already a champion at two in 1947, Calumet Farm's Citation came out at three as a dominating force seldom matched. He won nineteen of twenty races, and his tour of the Triple Crown was accomplished with such ease that jockey Eddie Arcaro pronounced him the best horse he ever rode.

After Citation, a peculiar thing happened to the Triple Crown. If it had been important while being won frequently, it would become an obsession while being left untouched. For twenty-five years, a succession of great horses tried and failed, several felled by ill luck or unsoundness or lack of stamina. These included Native

AT RIGHT

Calumet Farm's glory days were epitomized by Citation's three-year-old campaign in 1948. Citation won nineteen of twenty races that year and convinced Eddie Arcaro that he was the best horse the great jockey had ever ridden. Courtesy Jerry Cooke.

Dancer, Nashua, Majestic Prince, Carry Back, Damascus, Tim Tam, and Northern Dancer. As the years passed and the drought of Triple Crown winners lengthened, many horsemen feared that the series was too tough in a time of massive expansion of the Thoroughbred population. Perhaps it would never be won again.

This timidity was washed away by Secretariat. Meadow Stable's Big Red of a newer era was so overpowering at two that voters made him Horse of the Year. At three, he had become the most expensive horse to that date, being syndicated for $6 million. Such were the expectations and such was the aura around him, that most horses would have fallen short. Instead, Secretariat exceeded even the most optimistic and romantic visions of what he might achieve.

Power and beauty lived in equal parts with his every stride as he rolled through the Churchill Down stretch to win his Derby in record time. He then turned

ABOVE
Kelso was Horse of the Year five times, more often than any other horse in history. He swept New York's Handicap Triple,
a feat matched before and after only by Whisk Broom II, Tom Fool, and Fit to Fight.

in a similar performance in Pimlico's Preakness. Ahead lay the Belmont, the Achilles' heel of Triple Crown pretenders. Since Citation, a half-dozen colts had won the first two jewels of the crown, only to come up short in the Belmont Stakes. Secretariat turned the challenge into an exhibition. He burst into an early lead with such lavish speed that he seemed destined to tire in the daunting final furlongs of the 1½–mile test. Rather than weaken, however, he seemed to gain momentum, as if each furlong pole launched him anew. Through the glorious final half-minute of the Belmont, he transcended witnesses' experience, drawing farther and farther ahead until he won by thirty-one lengths. He had run 1 1/4 miles faster than his own Kentucky Derby record and yet sped on the remaining quarter-mile to hang up a final time of 2:24—a world record for the distance.

After so many years of Triple Crown draught, only four years later Seattle Slew won it while undefeated, and then the next year Affirmed turned back Alydar three times to become the eleventh and last Triple Crown winner.

Greatness as expressed by the likes of Man o' War and Secretariat is precocious and obvious. Another type of greatness is that of the gallant campaigner with us year after year, perhaps slower to develop but enthralling in a different way. The epitome of that type of career was Kelso, a gelding that emerged in the summer of his three-year-old season and then took American racing in his grasp for half the decade. Mrs. Richard C. du Pont's angular veteran carried up to 136 pounds as he defeated wave after wave of younger horses. Eventually, he was Horse of the Year five times (1960–1964), an unprecedented achievement.

Very much like the career of Kelso was that of Forego, another gelding, winner of the 1976 Marlboro Cup under 137 pounds and Horse of the Year three times. Similar campaigns endeared geldings Armed

and Exterminator and the future stallions Seabiscuit and Stymie to the American racing fan.

For the most part, great horses bear pedigrees that at least hint at license for exceptional success. Yet, one of the lures of the turf is the lurking opportunity for the lowly to emerge. The life of John Henry bore such a stamp. Once sold for as little as $1,100, John Henry wound up as the one-horse stable for self-made businessman Sam Rubin. He took the concept of improving with age to new levels. John Henry was Horse of the Year for the first time at six and was the champion again at nine. By the time of his retirement, the once obscure little gelding had won thirty-nine races and $6.5 million.

Like their male counterparts, champion fillies and mares express their qualities in a variety of patterns. American racing has loved the elegant, feminine forms of Top Flight and Busher, the ruggedness of Gallorette and Shuvee as they challenged males, and the sheer quality of Twilight Tear, Ruffian, Personal Ensign, and Go for Wand.

Gallorette and Personal Ensign provide examples of differing poles of greatness. Gallorette's trump card was an incredible durability. The Maryland-bred daughter of Challenger II raced for her breeder, W. L. Brann. The mating that produced her, however, came on the advice of trainer Preston Burch. The latter had spotted the fashionably bred Gallette, then relegated to the hunt fields. Burch was not fortunate enough to train the result of the first Challenger II–Gallette mating. That foal, Gallorette, went to the stable of Ed Christmas.

Gallorette raced from two through six, retiring in 1948 with earnings of $445,535, then a record for her sex. She won twenty-one races in seventy-two starts, and, in addition to winning a sequence of the better distaff races, she battled year after year with such distinguished male handicappers as Stymie, Assault, Armed, and Pavot. In one of her most memorable moments, she was passed by the typical stretch drive of the powerful

Stymie, but gathered herself to come back at him and win by a neck in the 1946 Brooklyn Handicap. In 1950, Delaware Park held a vote among a group of writers to name the best filly or mare in the first half of the twentieth century. The winner was Gallorette.

By contrast, Personal Ensign earned her fame with less racing, but unbroken success. Trainer Shug McGaughey had Ogden Phipps's Private Account filly ready for the Breeders' Cup at two after victory in the Frizette, but a leg fracture ended her juvenile campaign and threatened her career. She was back, unbeaten again at three before another long layoff. At four, Personal Ensign was still perfection, reeling off facile wins in the Hempstead and Beldame and defeating males in the Whitney. In the thirteenth and final race of her career, she seemed at sea in the off track at Churchill Downs, but made an amazing drive up the stretch to catch Winning Colors in time to conclude her career without a single loss. She had earned $1,679,880.

So, a great Thoroughbred may be male or female, precocious or late to achieve, patrician or pedestrian. Each has the power to stir mankind's highest sporting instincts, to bring a cheering crowd to its feet, to embed memories and affections that live on long after the echoes have lilted to the heavens.

AT RIGHT
After twenty-five years without a Triple Crown winner, Secretariat turned the climactic Belmont Stakes into a moment of national celebration.
Courtesy New York Racing Association.

THE GREAT BLOODLINES

Backstage from the excitement of the racetrack are the cadences of the breeding farm. The stewardship of the Thoroughbred's genetic destinies has long been a central role played by mankind in his relationship with the animal. As with any breed, tracing the origins and setting guidelines for inclusion was an administrative component to accompany the genetics of the evolving breed.

Inasmuch as transportation, farming, and warfare had been the horse's overriding roles in civilization, it is not surprising that the beginning of the development of racehorses was seen in a dual light. When Governor Nicolls of

AT LEFT

The eight-time leading stallion Bold Ruler was depicted by noted artist Richard Stone Reeves, surrounded by eleven of his progeny which were named champions. Courtesy Ogden Phipps.

New York had a racecourse laid out on Long Island in 1665, he specified that the effort was "not so much for the divertisement of youth as for encouraging the betterment of the improvement of the breed of horses, which through great neglect has been impaired."

The concept of "improving the breed" was so inherent in the early thinking that it became something of a cliche, finally being affixed whimsically to the recreation of betting on horses. Eventually, of course, the role of horses in everyday commerce, society, and warfare would diminish, creating the luxury of seeking to breed racehorses for the singular purpose of racing. This endeavor has attracted divergent personalities embracing science, theory, economic ambition, sportsmanship, and aesthetics.

Governor Nicolls's course was created only five years after Charles II's restoration to the throne reinvigorated the English turf. A year earlier, the British had ended Dutch rule in New Amsterdam, renamed it New York, and installed Nicolls as governor.

Mother England during that century was busy with many matters, and one was the establishment of the Thoroughbred breed. A motley amalgam of exotic imports from the Orient, speedy little Irish hobbies, and native mares were worked into this scheme. Far across the Atlantic, the colonists were quick to imitate their brethren from the homeland, as they did in all matters wherein it pleased them to do so.

The distances between towns, the various climates, and the economics of life in America created unique flavors for racing on this side of the Atlantic. For breeding stock, however, Americans looked to England, both before and after the Revolutionary War. Thus, the American Thoroughbred developed along a sort of patchwork pattern and, while for many years American strains were not

ABOVE

The gravestone of Domino at Mt. Brilliant, Lexington, Kentucky, extolls him as "the fleetest runner the American Turf has ever known."
In the 1890s, there would have been few who disagreed. Courtesy *The Blood-Horse*.

recognized in England's General Stud Book, the quality of American racing stock evolved satisfactorily.

A common scenario was an English stallion at the fountainhead of what became known in time as an "American" line. Toward the end of the nineteenth century, American lines included those of Domino, Hindoo, Hastings, and Lexington. The line of Hastings, sire of Fair Play, reached its peak in the latter's son, Man o' War, begetter of such as War Admiral, Crusader, and War Relic. This line, so precious in history, survives today, its recent generations being represented by such as In Reality, Relaunch, Olden Times, and Known Fact.

The line of the great racer Domino, son of Himyar, is another of the old American lines still extant. Its existence has been tenuous, its resilience remarkable. Domino, a

whirlwind of the 1890s, sired only nineteen foals before his death. Fortunately, one of these was Commando, a champion racehorse, but likewise limited at stud, getting only twenty-seven foals. The tendency for this bloodline's destiny to hang by a genetic thread carried on to Commando's unbeaten son Colin. A shy breeder, Colin sired eighty-one foals in twenty-three crops, and none were comparable as racehorses to their best forebears.

Nevertheless, there was a single individual in each generation to carry the line into the 1990s. Alsab and later Ack Ack were champions among those in that chain, and, ironically, Ack Ack was the vehicle for this narrow channel's flow back into the founding land. His son Youth was a champion in France and later sired Teenoso, winner of that most seminal of horse races, the Epsom Derby in England.

ABOVE

Commando's owner, James R. Keene, had not been impressed by his dam and was so skeptical over the prospects of the colt that he declined to nominate him to the Futurity. Nevertheless, trainer James Rowe, Sr., found nine other races for him, of which Commando won all but two. Courtesy *The Blood-Horse*.

When one addresses the great and flourishing bloodlines, the importance of frequent importations is recognized as profound. As the era of jet travel replaced the days of difficult voyages on the high seas, the intermingling became so commonplace that national designations are less meaningful today even than they were in the past. Nevertheless, the wellspring of the modern Thoroughbred remains England and Ireland; even those lines that in recent generations are regarded as French or Italian were but few generations from an English export.

The most extraordinary and lasting influence in the present century was launched by the sprinter Phalaris. Of the bellwether stallions of this century, Nearco, Nasrullah, Bold Ruler, Hail to Reason, Mill Reef, Native Dancer, Raise a Native, Mr. Prospector, and Northern Dancer all trace in direct male line to Phalaris.

Phalaris himself, however, seemed ill-equipped to author such a noble heritage. He was bred by the seventeenth Lord Derby, whose father had resurrected the family's interest in the turf. Lord Derby's trainer, George Lambton, had a successful record, but there came a time when he felt a fresh influx of speed and ruggedness was needed in the owner's breeding stock. He recommended purchase of the mare Bromus, closely inbred to the speedy Springfield. When bred to Polymelus, sire of three Epsom Derby winners, Bromus produced Phalaris. The latter was a high-class horse, but was stretched to get ten furlongs. Despite the recognition on the part of his advisers that more speed was needed in his breeding program, Lord Derby clung to the old thought that a Derby winner and an Oaks winner (both races at 1 1/2 miles) was the ideal pattern. Thus, he would have sold Phalaris if he had been able to, but World War I was being fought at the time, and the bloodstock market was cramped. Reluctantly given a chance as a stallion, Phalaris got a number of sons of lasting influence. Today, lines through two of them, Pharos and Sickle, are still dominant.

Like Lord Derby, Italy's Federico Tesio was one of the influential breeders of the twentieth century, although the Italian horseman had much less financial wherewithal than the nobleman. By careful selection of English stock, Tesio had bred upward several families, and in Nearco, son of Pharos, he bred an undefeated international champion and a sire of surpassing quality. Nearco's sons included the willful Nasrullah that Bull Hancock of Claiborne Farm imported to Kentucky and thereby established an American branch of profound importance. Nasrullah's best sons included Bold Ruler, the dashing champion for Wheatley Stable that later led America's sire list eight times and begot the superb Triple Crown winner Secretariat. (Another Triple Crown winner, Seattle Slew, also traces to Bold Ruler in the direct male line.) Nashua, Jaipur, Noor, Indian Hemp (sire of leading sire T. V. Lark), Grey Sovereign, and Red God also were by Nasrullah. Yet another son was Never Bend, he in turn the sire of Riverman and of Paul Mellon's Epsom Derby and Prix de l'Arc de Triomphe winner, Mill Reef.

Nor was Nasrullah the only author of importance in America for the Nearco line. Nearco also sired Royal Charger. Charger's son Turn-to was responsible for the lines that led to Sir Gaylord, Sir Ivor, Hail to Reason, Roberto, Halo, and Sunday Silence.

There was still more in the legacy of Nearco, and again it connected to Lord Derby. Another of the great horses bred by Lord Derby was Hyperion, an influential horse in this country that provided the dam of Citation, the Kentucky Derby winner Pensive, and the leading sire Heliopolis. In 1952, E.

ABOVE

Colin was one of many champions exercised by noted horseman Marshall Lilly. In the days before mandatory helmets, morning hat wear on the racetrack was left to personal taste. Lilly was partial to his derby. Photograph by C. C. Cook. Courtesy Keeneland-Cook.

P. Taylor asked George Blackwell to purchase for him the best mare at the Newmarket December sale, and Blackwell secured Lady Angela, a Hyperion mare, for 10,500 guineas. He also arranged for her to be returned to Nearco.

Taylor, the entrepreneur who amalgamated Canada's brewing industry as well as its Thoroughbred sport, was determined to prove he could produce world-class horses at his Windfields Farm in Ontario. Lady Angela was imported to Windfields and there foaled her Nearco colt Nearctic, later to become his country's Horse of the Year. Nearctic's first crop included Northern Dancer, winner of the Kentucky Derby and Preakness before heading into the most influential stallion career of the last third of the century, and the horse that completed Taylor's crusade.

There is still more of Lord Derby and of Phalaris to this saga. Northern Dancer was out of a daughter of Native Dancer, the great gray that won twenty-one of twenty-two races. Native Dancer was by Polynesian, a horse that went back to Phalaris, via Sickle.

Northern Dancer sired more than 140 stakes winners, including Nijinsky II and two other Epsom Derby winners, plus Lyphard, Nureyev, and Danzig. His are the most predominant issue in the world as the twentieth century wanes, and his blood was instrumental in the shift of transatlantic traffic that saw European stables buying top-priced yearlings from the former "colonies."

Northern Dancer's maternal grandsire, Native Dancer, also sired the brilliant Raise a Native, thus establishing another branch

ABOVE

Smithson Broadhead substituted himself and his wife in the background of his portrait of Nashua after the colt's owner, William Woodward, Jr., was killed by Mrs. Woodward in a society cause celebre. Also depicted are trainer Sunny Jim Fitzsimmons and jockey Eddie Arcaro. Courtesy National Museum of Racing.

AT RIGHT

Alfred Vanderbilt's Native Dancer, the "Gray Ghost" of early televised racing, was a lasting international influence, as sire of Raise a Native and grandsire of Northern Dancer and Sea-Bird II. Painting by Richard Stone Reeves.

of the Phalaris dynasty. That branch includes twice-leading sire Mr. Prospector; leading sire Alydar; Triple Crown winner Affirmed; Horse of the Year Alysheba; and the champion Easy Goer. The bounty of Phalaris, though distant, has not been depleted.

During the 1940s and 1950s, Bull Lea played a role similar to that later taken on by Bold Ruler and then by Northern Dancer. Bull Lea led the sire list five times and was largely responsible for the dynasty of his owner, Calumet Farm. Each spring brought the presumption that several of the top classic prospects would be sons of Bull Lea. Among them were three Kentucky Derby winners—Citation, Iron Liege, and Hill Gail—as well as Coaltown, General Duke, and the filly Twilight Tear.

Bull Lea traced to another earlier import, and, again, the intermediary was but a few generations removed from England. Bull Lea was a son of Bull Dog, son of the French-bred Teddy. Edmond Blanc, a leading French breeder, had purchased the 1899 English Triple Crown winner Flying Fox and with him bred the brilliant Ajax. The latter sired Teddy, sold by Blanc as a yearling as the Germans were approaching Paris. Purchased by J. D. Cohn, Teddy raced in Spain before returning to France to win at four. He got Bull Dog (sire of Bull Lea) when mated with Plucky Liege, one of the key broodmares of the century. Another mating of Teddy and Plucky Liege produced Sir Gallahad III, imported to Claiborne and leader of the sire list four times. Sir Gallahad III sired Gallant Fox, the 1930 Triple Crown winner for William Woodward, Sr.'s, Belair Stud.

Another French mare, of even more influence than Plucky Liege, was La Troienne, bred by the masterful Marcel Boussac. La Troienne was imported for Colonel E. R. Bradley, who, like the Hancocks and Hal Price Headley, was a proponent of crossing European and American blood. Bradley could not afford to import the best European horses, but he went for lesser fillies from

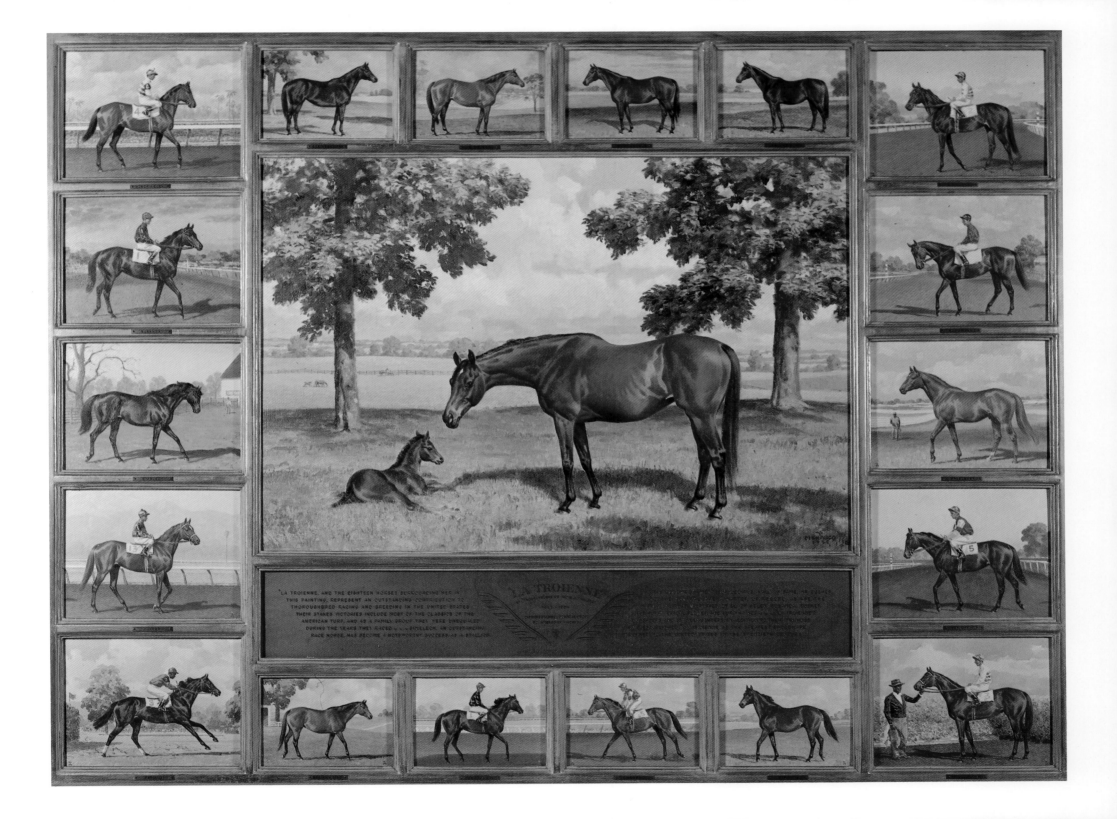

top families. La Troienne produced five major winners. After the breakup of Idle Hour Stock Farm following Colonel Bradley's death in 1946, daughters and granddaughters of the mare were instrumental in the success of Ogden Phipps's, Greentree Stud's, and The King Ranch's breeding operations. Among her legion of distinguished descendants was Phipps's superb Buckpasser, a champion every year he raced (1965–1967).

At the time The Jockey Club was created in 1894, Hanover had been the leading sire of his era. Racing then proceeded through the supremacy of Star Shoot and Broomstick, and breeders such as John E. Madden and Harry Payne Whitney. Next came Belair Stud and Calumet Farm, in the days of imported sires Sir Gallahad III and Blenheim II, in addition to Bull Lea. The overwhelming Nasrullah–Bold Ruler stage came next, touching many private and commercial horsemen while Bieber-Jacobs Stable had a run as leading breeder. The

great stallion Ribot, bred by Italy's masterful Federico Tesio, was a contemporary of international significance.

Lastly has been the Northern Dancer and Raise a Native influence, while Taylor's Windfields, Elmendorf Farm, Nelson Bunker Hunt, Phipps, Tartan Farm, Kinghaven, and Sam-Son Farms of Canada took turns ascending to the top of the breeders' list. The 1992 season underscored the international themes now extant, when California breeders Mr. and Mrs. John Mabee led the North American owners' list over runner-up Juddmonte Farm, the American entity in the vast Thoroughbred holdings of Prince Khaled Abdullah of Saudi Arabia.

As always, the ebb and flow of bloodlines has been only partially the product of visionary breeders and businessmen. For the most part, the destinies of bloodlines are the work of unharnessed forces within nature. Breeding theories and knowledge abound, but the mysteries of genetics confound those who would seek the formula for certain success.

AT RIGHT

Mr. Prospector was primarily a sprinter, but his progeny have proven superb at a variety of distances as he has become a multiple-year leading sire. Originally at stud in Florida, he later was moved to Claiborne Farm in Kentucky. Photograph by Dell Hancock.

TURF PERSONALITIES

When Jimmy Cagney hoofed through George M. Cohan's lyrics in the movie *Yankee Doodle Dandy* on his way to an Oscar in 1942, he entrenched more deeply in history the legend of jockey Tod Sloan. Cagney was eight years old when Sloan, on whom his Yankee Doodle character was based, strolled into the office of James R. Keene, the "Silver Fox" of Wall Street, to unveil his intention of riding one of Keene's horses in England.

As later recounted by Keene's son, Foxhall Keene: "On a day in September 1897, a person dressed in what can be described only as a flaming raiment, with a cigar a foot long between his teeth, strolled nonchalantly past

AT LEFT

In addition to owning the likes of Discovery and Native Dancer, Alfred Vanderbilt (left) answered the challenge of leadership as head of tracks in Maryland and New York. He presents a trophy here to owner Royce Martin and jockey Conn McCreary. Photograph by Pimlico Photo Service. Courtesy *The Blood-Horse*.

an over-awed secretary, right into my father's private office. 'I'm Tod Sloan,' he announced to my astonished parent, 'and I want to ride St. Cloud in the Cesarewitch and Cambridgeshire.'"

James Forman Sloan was known as Tod, a nickname given him by his father back in Kokomo, Indiana. (He later assumed the middle name of Todhunter, hinting at a grander origin of his nickname.) From his midwestern roots, he set out on a life of odd jobs and carnival stunts, winding up at the racetrack. In 1894, the same year The Jockey Club was taking the boardroom route to reshaping its aspects of the turf, Sloan, the obscure rider, slipped out of his straight-legged Victorian purchase on a horse in California. Crouching

with some desperation over the beast's neck, Sloan nevertheless recognized that the animal was running more freely than usual. Thus was born the short-stirrup seat that carried Sloan to fame as "monkey on a stick."

In six seasons, Sloan swaggered his way to racing victories and high living at the best racecourses in America and England. The cigar, a "foot long," that amused the Messrs. Keene was a trademark, as was his arrogance whether he was ordering champagne and caviar at the best hotels and casinos or ignoring instructions proffered in the paddock by the best English trainers. Sloan rode for Lily Langtry and the Prince of Wales (Edward VII), utilizing a style that later was taken to the extremes of today's jockeys. In the end, however, his arrogance was more than the English could

ABOVE
Dapper Tod Sloan, with ever-present cigar, became the toast of English racing with a style commonly called "monkey on a stick."
He presaged a wave of success for American riders in the late nineteenth and early twentieth centuries. Courtesy *The Blood-Horse*.

AT RIGHT
The dramatis personae of the turf has always had its share of colorful characters. Diamond Jim Brady was more than a flamboyant figure playing the tracks.
He also owned the good horse Oiseau in the early 1900s. Photograph by C. C. Cook. Courtesy Keeneland-Cook.

stand, especially when it became known that he gambled on his mounts. He was eventually denied a license. Afterward, he knocked around the world for three more decades, during which his friend Cohan wrote him into stage and film history as "Little Johnny Jones."

Delete the tragic aspects (sometimes), and the life of Sloan is a prototype for many American riders. The dead-end kid determination to rise above poor circumstances and diminutive stature were indeed hallmarks of the early days of many riders. Among them were champions like Eddie Arcaro, Earl Sande, George (The Iceman) Woolf, Johnny Longden, and Bill (Willie the Shoe) Shoemaker, who was so tiny at birth that doctors despaired of his surviving the night. Shoemaker's grandmother placed him in a shoe box and used the oven as an incubator!

Eddie Arcaro was the most famous rider of the 1940s and 1950s. Banana Nose, as he was called affectionately, was once banned from racing for a year, after

ABOVE
Pierre Lorillard was a pillar of racing and also influenced clothing fashion. Gentlemen's attire at formal dinners at his Tuxedo Park lent its name to the uniforms of generations of headwaiters and self-conscious prom lads. Photograph by MESSY, Nice. Courtesy Keeneland Library.

he admitted that he had intentionally committed a foul to get revenge on another jockey.

Arcaro was regarded as the best rider for big races, and the parade of champions he partnered regularly included Whirlaway, Citation, Nashua, Kelso, and Sword Dancer. He set a record by winning five Kentucky Derbys (matched only by Bill Hartack) and also won six Preaknesses and six Belmonts. Arcaro retired in 1961, with 4,779 wins. His career earnings of some $30 million was a record at the time, although by the 1980s top riders were soaring past the $100 million mark.

Bill Hartack was the antithesis of the smooth, low-crouching rider who seems almost a part of his horse. By his own admission, Hartack resembled "a sack of manure" when riding, but he had a determination and a rapport with horses that made him a champion. Early on in his career Hartack had problems with the press because he insisted "don't call me Willie." Moreover, he was ruthlessly honest with owners and trainers, telling

ABOVE
August Belmont II bred Man o' War, but sold him when World War I supply efforts called Belmont abroad.
Belmont also was a major financier of the first New York subway. Courtesy *The Blood-Horse.*

them after a race if a horse had not been well prepared or, simply, was not good enough. Occasionally, he had horses scratched at the post because he felt they were not sound enough to race. While those actions certainly protected him, the horse, all the other riders, and the betting public, such incidents embarrassed trainers and owners.

Hartack had a brilliant record in the Derby, winning five times on his first nine mounts, but as a young rider he denied placing any special importance on the great event—one more nettle to the press and horsemen alike. His Derby winners were Iron Liege (1957), Venetian Way (1960), Decidedly (1962), Northern Dancer (1964), and Majestic Prince (1969).

Hartack's final Derby winner, Majestic Prince, was trained by another great rider, John Longden. Longden was among many top jockeys raised in

Canada, the others including Ted Atkinson and Sandy Hawley. Longden passed Sir Gordon Richards as the world-leading rider in victories, and, in a final flourish, won the 1966 San Juan Capistrano on Canadian-bred George Royal for the last ride of his career.

By the 1950s, owner-breeder Fred W. Hooper began looking south of the border for riders. Hooper, a self-made Southerner who won the Kentucky Derby with one of his first horses, Hoop, Jr., spotted talent in Panama. Manuel Ycaza, Braulio Baeza, and Laffit Pincay, Jr., thus came north, a trend that would continue for Hispanic riders. From the Caribbean and South America came other jockeys with skill and flash— Avelino Gomez, Jorge Velasquez, Jacinto Vasquez, Jose Santos, and the irrepressible Angel Cordero, Jr. The Hall of Fame became bilingual.

ABOVE

The many distinguished racing figures in uniform during World War II included John Hay (Jock) Whitney (right), who once leapt from a P.O.W. train to escape imprisonment. Here he presents the 1945 Belmont Stakes trophy to Pavot's owner, Walter M. Jeffords, Sr. (left), attended by George D. Widener and jockey Eddie Arcaro. Photograph by Bert Morgan. Courtesy *The Blood-Horse.*

AT RIGHT

On a bright summer day in 1930, Saratoga president George Bull greeted Governor and Mrs. Franklin Roosevelt. Later that day, the skies darkened, and the track was drenched with rain by the time Jim Dandy raced to an historic upset in the Travers Stakes. Photograph by C. C. Cook. Courtesy George S. Bolster Collection of the Historical Society of Saratoga Springs.

Steve Cauthen was the sensational kid of America in 1978, when he won the Triple Crown with Affirmed. Cauthen then followed Tod Sloan's example with championship seasons in England. Cauthen became the gentleman Sloan had sought to be. Likewise, Pat Day, Eddie Delahoussaye, and Chris McCarron are among riders who have forged great careers with style, not swagger, while Julie Krone broke down many of the barriers against women who want to become jockeys.

In the pulse of a youngish America on the move, in the late nineteenth century and early twentieth century, the rough-and-tumble route to success on the racetrack went hand-in-glove with the fortune-makers of Wall Street, manufacturing, gold, silver, iron, copper, tobacco, and oil.

For example, William Collins Whitney made so much money in public transportation, utilities, and tobacco, that when he turned to racing he had the wherewithal to spruce up the old racetrack at Saratoga. One of his trainers was Sam Hildreth, part Indian, a self-made horseman who was America's leading trainer nine times.

In a later era, when the straightlaced, conservative Warren Wright, Sr., owned many of America's best horses under the banner of Calumet Farm, his trainer was Ben A. Jones, abetted by son Jimmy. Jones, a Missourian, had grown up poor, scuffling along at rowdy tracks back when "I had to win in a hurry, because I needed money living day to day." One of the stories Kentucky hardboot-farm-manager Olin Gentry loved to tell about his old friend Jones was the time Pancho Villa's boys were requisitioning horses at the old Tijuana track, without bothering with paperwork. Jones put mud packs on the legs of one of his best horses to make him look lame. Villa's gang was duly fooled. Jones set a record by training six Kentucky Derby winners, including Whirlaway and Citation.

Patrician banker and chairman of The Jockey Club, William Woodward, Sr., had as trainer Sunny Jim

Fitzsimmons, an ex-jockey whose back was bent from the days of sweating at a brick kiln in order to keep his riding weight down. Texan Robert Kleberg, Jr., the genetics and ranching genius of the King Ranch, employed Max Hirsch, another ex-jockey, who had ridden against Tod Sloan. Secretariat, owned by the family of distinguished industrialist Christopher T. Chenery, was trained by Lucien Lauren, a French Canadian who had ridden in the rag-tag days of short-race meetings on the Montreal circuits. Captain Harry Guggenheim, of a family noted in business and the arts and himself a pioneer in aerospace, had years of success with Woody Stephens, a garrulous ex-rider who later won five consecutive runnings of the Belmont Stakes, including two for Henryk de Kwiatkowski, the flamboyant Polish airplane dealer who swooped into the Bluegrass in 1992 to purchase the proud jewel known as Calumet Farm.

Beneath any successful trainer's veneer is the steel to withstand a struggle, for the day-to-day life and its

ABOVE

Colonel E. R. Bradley developed Idle Hour Farm in Kentucky and won four Kentucky Derbys. Liz Whitney-Tippett had Llangollen Farm divisions in Virginia, Florida, California, and New York. Her best horses included Porterhouse and Pretense. Photography by Bert and Richad Morgan. Courtesy *The Blood-Horse*.

pressures are tough. Even those with a leg up must be hard and relentless workers to succeed, so that even sons and grandsons in families such as the Burches, Veitches, Jolleys, Hirsches, Jerkenses, and Whittinghams have to prove themselves by their own work. A pedigree alone does not win races, either for horses or people. The Latin trainers, such as Horatio Luro, Laz Barrera, and Angel Penna, might have projected an aura of well-being, but they had their turns hustling and scuffling, to go with the charm.

Charlie Whittingham, once Luro's assistant and partner, typifies the intensity and concentration of the great horseman. For the most part, trainers prefer owners who leave decisions to the man at the barn. In this

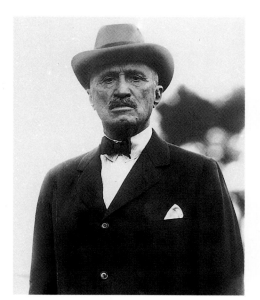

ABOVE, LEFT TO RIGHT
Racing leaders of their time: Richard Wilson and Mrs. Averell Harriman; John E. Madden of Hamburg Place; William Woodward, Sr., of Belair Stud, and Arthur B. Hancock, Sr., of Claiborne Farm. Courtesy *The Blood-Horse* and Keeneland-Cook.

light, Whittingham has often said that treating owners is like handling mushrooms: "Keep them in the dark and spread the manure on them."

LeRoy Jolley is the son of hardboot-horseman Moody Jolley, one of those of a generation that, the son says, "didn't have much give-up in them." In his twenties, LeRoy saddled the powerful, but erratic Ridan, beaten in both the Derby and Preakness. By 1975, he had won his first Derby, with Foolish Pleasure, and in 1980 he won it again with the filly Genuine Risk.

The history of racing and breeding is distinguished by many of America's greatest families such as the three generations (and counting) of the Phippses, plus the Whitneys, Vanderbilts, Belmonts, Wideners, Schiffs, Guests, Bancrofts, Farishes, Jeffords, Galbreaths, and others. The ultrawealthy, however, are widely outnumbered by owners of more modest backgrounds. The spell of racing might be no stronger to a Paul Mellon, philanthropist and aesthete, than to a Jack Price, a midwestern businessman who bred Carry Back from a mare he accepted in lieu of a board bill and decided to train the horse himself. Price won the Kentucky Derby with Carry Back.

California has spawned many successful racing operations. The leading owner in North America in 1992 and a record-setting breeder, with twenty-five stakes winners in 1991, was the Golden Eagle Ranch of California. Golden Eagle is owned by Mr. and Mrs. John Mabee, transplanted Iowans. Mabee established a chain of grocery stores and then expanded into other businesses. He not only operates a breeding operation that has turned out the likes of Best Pal and River Special, but he has been a prime shaper of the sport in Southern California as head of Del Mar racetrack.

As would be true of most pursuits with formal origins dating from the 1600s, Thoroughbred racing through much of history has been dominated by men.

ON PREVIOUS PAGE
Jockey Eddie Arcaro confers with trainer Sunny Jim Fitzsimmons. The two teamed for many major triumphs in the 1950s, with Nashua and then Bold Ruler. Photograph by Jerry Cooke.

AT RIGHT
Jockey Bill Shoemaker became a racing hero in the 1940s and by the time of his retirement in 1990 had won a record 8,833 races.
He since has succeeded as a trainer despite a highway accident that consigned him to a wheelchair. Photograph by Norman Mauskopf.

Nevertheless, women have played a strong role, as owners, breeders, trainers, and jockeys. The prominent women in American racing during the last century have included such formidable aristocrats as Mrs. Payne Whitney and her daughter Joan Whitney Payson of Greentree Stable, Mrs. Henry Carnegie Phipps of Wheatley Stable, Mrs. Lucille (Wright) Markey of Calumet, Mrs. Isabel Dodge Sloane of Brookmeade, and Mrs. Marion du Pont Scott of Montpelier in Virginia. More recently, women such as Liz Whitney-Tippett, Mary Jones Bradley, Frances Genter, Ada L. Rice, Alice Headley Chandler, Cynthia Phipps, Penny Chenery, Karen Taylor and Sally Hill, Viola Sommer, Jane Lunger, Allaire du Pont, Virginia Kraft Payson, and Helen Alexander have all been successful as breeders and owners.

Given that wagering is a part of the turf, it is not surprising that many of racing's most formidable characters were gamblers. Owner John Gates was known as Bet-A-Million because of his fondness for a wager, while Colonel E. R. Bradley once testified in Congress that gambling was his occupation. This was not, however, his only activity. Bradley's Idle Hour Stock Farm won four Kentucky Derbys and hosted charity race meetings for orphans.

Racing has often attracted the famous from other spheres, and Hollywood personalities have long been supporters of the turf, especially in California. Bing Crosby crooned to the crowd the day he and Pat O'Brien opened Del Mar, down on the surf outside San Diego, and Fred Astaire raced Gold Cup winner Triplicate at Hollywood Park in

ABOVE

Paul Mellon fell for Thoroughbreds, and England, at an early age. His gifts to society include numerous pieces of sporting art and places to house them, and his contributions to the Thoroughbred include the breeding of Mill Reef, Arts and Letters, and 1993 Kentucky Derby winner Sea Hero. Photograph by Dell Hancock.

1946. More recently, Cary Grant, Telly Savalas, John Forsythe, Elizabeth Taylor, Mickey Rooney, Tim Conway, Kevin Costner, and producer Ray Stark have been among celebrities with ownership in racehorses.

Not since Andrew Jackson have we had a President who stabled runners on White House property, but the government has not been without its distinguished participants in racing. When August Belmont II died in the 1920s, Averell Harriman and President Bush's grandfather bought his racing stable. Harriman, later a distinguished diplomat and governor of New York, raced 1927 champion runner Chance Play. In recent

decades, secretaries of the treasury Ogden Mills, George M. Humphrey, and Nicholas Brady have been prominent owners, as have other members of their families. (Brady was also chairman of The Jockey Club.) Also, owners C. V. Whitney and John W. Hanes held undersecretary posts in the cabinet, while John Hay (Jock) Whitney was Ambassador to the Court of St. James and William S. Farish of Lane's End Farm was a confidante of President Bush.

The social tapestry of the turf is a tribute to the multiple tentacles of its appeal. The racehorse is one common link among many people who otherwise might have none.

ABOVE

Early in his career, Mack Miller trained the precocious filly Leallah. Much of his later success, for owners Charles Engelhard and Paul Mellon, came with a more classic type of horse, including Sea Hero, Java Gold, Assagai, and Hawaii. Miller selected Fit to Fight for Mellon at the yearling sales and sent him out to sweep the New York Handicap Triple. Photograph by Dell Hancock.

1 8 9 4 – 1 9 2 0

In 1894 American Thoroughbred racing was a haphazard collage, a combination of a carnival and an opera. The grandness of the New York courses, such as Morris Park and Jerome Park, bore only incidental resemblance to the ramshackle tracks strewn across the country in every state then in existence. Racing in those days had virtually no structure. In 1891 Pierre Lorillard launched an attempt to organize the American turf, establishing a body called the Board of Control. The board sought to replace local rules with uniform rules of racing, and created licensing procedures for jockeys and trainers.

Without such direction, racing might have smothered itself in overlap-

AT LEFT

Prior to the 1919 Kentucky Derby, Sir Barton had never won a race and was considered a pacemaker for stablemate Billy Kelly.
Instead, he led throughout, launching the first Triple Crown. Trainer Guy Bedwell is at his bridle, and John Loftus is aboard. Courtesy *The Blood-Horse*.

ping racing dates, for by the end of the 1880s no fewer than 314 racetracks were doing business in the United States, along with 43 in Canada.

By 1893, the Board of Control was coming under criticism of a sort that has been echoed across the following century. It was seen to be controlled by the racetracks, without proper representation of the viewpoints of owners of racing stables. Matters came to a head when James R. Keene was apprised of the tracks' intentions of reducing prize money.

In 1894, The Jockey Club was formed, with the purpose of taking control of racing. Its first chairman was John Hunter. The fifty-member club adopted the same name as England's prototype, begun around 1750 and named at a time when "jockey" meant someone having to do with horses, rather than having the specific definition of a rider in races. In 1895, the mantle of chairmanship of The Jockey Club was passed to August Belmont II, and there it resided until his death in 1924. Belmont thus became the most powerful individual on the American turf, and The Jockey Club established its Rules of Racing as the standards to be followed by all jurisdictions choosing to adopt them. The organization also participated in setting racing dates, at least insofar as eastern tracks were concerned, and established a fund to care for disabled trainers and jockeys. It began publishing the *Racing Calendar* as the official record, and, having sought to supervise the registration of Thoroughbreds since its founding, in 1896 the club took over the *American Stud Book*. Sanders D. Bruce compiled the pedigrees of American racehorses and published the first *Stud Book* in 1868. With its acquisition, The Jockey Club solidified its responsibility for the integrity of the breed in North America.

Even casual racing fans have heard the name Belmont, for it long ago was affixed to one of the coun-

ON PREVIOUS PAGE

Prior to the adoption of the pari-mutuel system, bookmakers lined the rails of racetracks. They took the betting action, then leapt onto four-legged stools to watch the races.
Photograph by J. C. Hemment. Courtesy Keeneland Library.

try's enduring classic races as well as one of her grandest racetracks. August Belmont II was the son of a brilliant businessman who had ascended so quickly in the Rothschilds banking offices in Europe, that when he arrived in New York in 1837 he soon had his own bank, with the Rothschilds as his major client.

Belmont had become a major owner and breeder by the time of his death in 1890, and August II went even farther. The son bred 129 stakes winners, and his champions included the great filly Beldame, winner of 12 of 14 races at three in 1904. Belmont was instrumental in establishing the underground transit system in New York City, and along with J. P. Morgan and William Collins Whitney, he built Belmont Park. While other tracks, like Jerome Park and Morris Park, had been grand, Belmont surpassed anything yet built. Belmont Park, wrote turf historian John Hervey in *Racing in America*, was "a revelation. People were in ecstasies over it." The track remains one of the bulwarks of the turf,

having been rebuilt and remodeled after a 1917 fire and then renovated on a grand scale after being condemned in the 1960s.

August Belmont II's greatest achievement as a horseman was the breeding of Man o' War. Ironically, he did not get to see the storied Big Red in his own colors, but he often nagged the colt's owner, Samuel Riddle, about the horse's management, as if he still owned him.

At the age of sixty-five, Belmont accepted a military commission to go to Spain in charge of procuring supplies for the Allies during World War I. He decided then to sell his yearling crop of 1918 and thus Man o' War was sent to Saratoga, where Riddle outbid Robert L. Gerry to buy him for $5,000 (the sale averaged $1,038). The colt had been named by Mrs. Belmont, the actress Eleanor Robson, who in later years was so instrumental in the Metropolitan Opera that her portrait today dominates the Belmont Room at Lincoln

Center. Belmont died in 1924, and his wife survived him by more than a half-century, living to 100.

While The Jockey Club brought some order where there had been chaos, its influence was not sufficient to stem a tide that rose to smash racing. This was a tide of ill-directed reform. To some extent, racing deserved the tarnished reputation it had been developing for too many decades. Bookmaking was legal then, and the presumption of widespread chicanery was probably not altogether inaccurate. Reformists of that period did not approve of gambling in the first place. A wave of legislation abolished racing in some of the states where it had been the best. New Jersey's grand Monmouth Park closed in 1893,

and others followed suit. By 1908, only twenty-five tracks in the United States and six in Canada were recognized, although numerous outlaw tracks still operated.

Chicago racing was curtailed after 1904. The most telling blow came in 1908, when New York Governor Charles Evans Hughes pushed through the Hart-Agnew Bill, making gambling illegal. Court action forestalled the shutdown for several years, but finally, in 1911 and 1912, there was no racing on the nation's primary circuit.

To an extent, the curtailment of racing in some states benefited others. Maryland, with its long tradition of racing, came to the fore again, with its circuit of Pimlico, Laurel, Havre de Grace, and Prince George Park (later called Bowie). Ontario for a time had the conti-

ABOVE

While English training was a matter of strings of horses spread over vast green heaths, centralized racing in America developed a different look and flavor. Here Beau Gallant whizzes through a morning work on a dirt track with the vast empty grandstand in the background. Photograph ky C. C. Cook. Courtesy Keeneland-Cook.

nent's leading purse structure, with its distinguished Woodbine course near the shores of Lake Ontario. In Kentucky, racing prospered.

An indirect result of the closing of some of the best racing was a fear abroad that there would be a flood of American horses and owners. As early as 1881, a breakthrough had occurred when Iroquois became the first American-bred to win the Epsom Derby. In 1908, the very year that Governor Hughes tried to end racing in New York, August Belmont II won one of England's five classic races, the Two Thousand Guineas, with an American-bred named Norman; Boss Croker of Tammany Hall won the One Thousand Guineas with Rhodora, daughter of an American mare. In France, William K. Vanderbilt won two of the historic races that year. There had already been a significant influx of American riders following the success of Tod Sloan of England.

England's response was not a forthright barrier, but the institution of the so-called Jersey Act. This involved tampering with *General Stud Book* requirements sufficiently to bar most American-breds from inclusion. The Jersey Act discouraged American horses from racing in England until 1949, when The Jockey Club's chairman, William Woodward, Sr., was instrumental in the act's amendment.

The tide of reform in the United States was short-lived. A New York court decision decreed that oral wagering arrangements "among friends" could not be made illegal. On May 30, 1913, some 35,000 turned out to greet the return of racing at Belmont Park. By the end of the decade, racing might have returned to America in full force, but the coming of World War I created yet another obstacle. The war was not as disruptive to racing as to many other aspects of life, but in 1918 the amount of activity on the American turf had fallen to 610 days whereas it had passed 1,000 in 1916.

On the surface, it seems that the quality of horses between the years 1894–1920 was impervious to the storms here and abroad. The presumption must be made that the restriction of foal crops and the diminution of the yearling market created fewer great horses, but the roll of champions is impressive.

The year 1894 saw a terrific series of duels between Henry of Navarre, Clifford, and Domino. Henry of Navarre emerged as the best of the three, but Domino was the most spectacular and remains the most remembered. Domino was bred in Kentucky by Major Barak Thomas, who had also bred his sire, the champion Himyar. Major Thomas sent Domino to the old Tattersall sale on Seventh Avenue in New York in 1893, where he was purchased as a yearling for $3,000 by Foxhall Keene. At two, Domino won all nine of his starts and earned $170,790, a record for two year olds until Top Flight's 1931 campaign.

Domino raced brilliantly again at three and four, retiring with a record of 19 wins in 25 starts. He stood at stud only two seasons at Castleton before dying. He was felled by spinal meningitis that was believed to have been caused by overfeeding, a somewhat common occurrence in his day. On his gravestone is engraved a sentiment touching the essence of man's love for the Thoroughbred: "Here lies the fleetest runner the American Turf has ever known, and one of the gamest and most generous of horses."

Domino, however, was only one of the great champions owned by the Keenes. Another was Sysonby, trained for James R. Keene by James R. Rowe, Sr. Sysonby is often grouped with Colin, Man o' War, Citation and Secretariat as the best of all time. Sysonby won fourteen of fifteen races in 1904 and 1905, and after his only defeat, to the filly Artful in the Futurity Stakes, a groom admitted to having drugged him to make him lose. In Sysonby's last race, the Great Republic Stakes at Saratoga, he defeated Diamond Jim Brady's Oiseau despite being left at the start. At four, Sysonby suffered an outbreak of a liver disease that proved fatal.

AT RIGHT

Jockeys casually await their turns to be weighed in the pleasant paddock area of Saratoga, in 1919. That summer, the Spa track saw the likes of Man o' War, Sir Barton, and Golden Broom. Photograph by H. C. Ashby. Courtesy George S. Bolster Collection of the Historical Society of Saratoga Springs.

Whether Sysonby was Keene's best horse is debatable, for the financier also bred and raced Colin. Few axioms are as safe as "they all get beat," but occasionally there have appeared horses that never lost. Colin was one, as were Europe's Ribot in the 1950s and the filly Personal Ensign in the 1980s.

Colin won all his 12 starts at two in 1907 for Keene and Rowe, then returned to win his 3 races at three. His next-to-last race was the Belmont Stakes, in which he defeated Fair Play, later to be renowned as the sire of Man o' War.

As noted earlier, Kentucky and Maryland were also centers of high-class racing. Colonel Matt Winn had created enough prestige for the Kentucky Derby that in 1915 Harry Payne Whitney sent his champion filly Regret there, declaring he would rather win it than any other race. Regret won

the Derby, and no other of her sex would win the great Churchill Downs race for sixty-five years.

Whitney was the son of William Collins Whitney, another versatile gatherer of wealth. Whitney had poured money into revitalizing the cherished racing at Saratoga Springs, the upstate New York spa and gambling town that had inaugurated its race meeting during the Civil War, in 1863. William Collins Whitney died in 1904, after only six years of heavy action on the turf. His stable was the leading owner three times, and his son, Harry Payne Whitney, was to lead the list six times before the mantle passed to his own son, C. V. Whitney. William Collins Whitney also was the father of Payne Whitney, whose wife launched Greentree Stud, an outfit still extant after two generations.

From early on, the Whitneys uti-

ABOVE

Harry Payne Whitney's Regret, Joe Notter aboard, became the first filly to win the Kentucky Derby, in 1915. As a broodmare, Regret was taken to a campfire by Whitney farm employees and honored in song the night another Whitney horse, Whiskery, won the Derby in 1927. Courtesy *The Blood-Horse*.

lized the advice of John E. Madden, the all-purpose horseman (trainer, breeder, owner, wheeler-dealer) who bred five Kentucky Derby winners. A grandson of Madden's, Preston Madden, extended the family history, continuing Hamburg Place, the arboreal farm that John E. established outside Lexington. In 1987, Alysheba became the sixth Derby winner bred at Hamburg Place.

Among the Derby winners bred by the original Madden was Sir Barton, a son of five-time leading sire Star Shoot. Madden sold Sir Barton for $10,000 to Canadian railroad tycoon J. K. L. Ross, for whom the colt swept what was to become the Triple Crown—the Derby, the Preakness, and the Belmont. The 1919 triumph came one year after the Derby victory of Exterminator, he to be beloved as Old Bones as he raced through 50 victories in 100 starts for patent-medicine salesman Willis Sharpe Kilmer.

Sir Barton's supremacy was short-lived, for the year he was a charging four year old, 1920, also brought out a burnished chestnut Fair Play colt, whose every aspect summoned drums and trumpets. The younger colt was Man o' War.

ABOVE, LEFT TO RIGHT

Three stars of the early twentieth century: The filly Artful, which won the 1904 Futurity for William Collins Whitney, founder of a racing dynasty; the gelding Old Rosebud, which won the 1914 Kentucky Derby and was still racing at eleven; and Whisk Broom II, which was returned from England in 1913 after the racing ban in New York was lifted and two weeks later won the Metropolitan Handicap. Courtesy *The Blood-Horse*.

1 9 2 0 – 1 9 4 0

For racing the Roaring Twenties began with Man o' War. Sam Riddle's chestnut colt swept aside all sent to face him, winning 11 in a row at three in 1920. He began with the Preakness Stakes, dashed through the Withers, and won the Belmont by twenty lengths. He later won the Lawrence Realization by 100 lengths, and eventually won The Jockey Club Stakes. (Later known as The Jockey Club Gold Cup, the event endures as one of Belmont Park's prized autumn races.)

For the Potomac Handicap, Man o' War's trainer Louis Feustel accepted an impost of 138 pounds. Man o' War gave thirty pounds to Wildair and beat

AT LEFT

Omaha was a son of Gallant Fox, and both were Triple Crown winners of the 1930s. An indifferent stallion, Omaha later was sent to the city of Omaha, Nebraska, and eventually was buried at the local race track, Ak-Sar-Ben. Painting by Martin Stainforth. Courtesy National Museum of Racing.

him 1½ lengths. After he beat Triple Crown winner Sir Barton in their match in Windsor, Ontario, Man o' War was retired, the Thoroughbred nonpareil. Most of Man o' War's stud career was spent at Lexington's Faraway Farm, owned by Walter Jeffords, Sr. Jeffords was a distinguished turfman, and his family has continued in that tradition.

Riddle used Man o' War as virtually a private stallion. This approach might have been fine had he possessed mares of equal quality. Such was far from the case, so Man o' War's success at stud was all the more remarkable. He begot American Flag, Crusader, Edith Cavell, and War Relic, in addition to Triple Crown winner War Admiral, and he led the American sire list in 1926. Man o' War died at thirty in 1947, and his funeral was widely broadcast by radio. He was buried at Faraway beneath Herbert Haseltine's heroic bronze likeness of him. Some thirty years later, the grave and statue were moved to Kentucky's new State Horse Park.

The year after Man o' War left the racetrack, the

ABOVE

Seabiscuit, a castoff from Wheatley Stable, became a star in California and upheld the prestige of western racing by defeating War Admiral in a match race
at Pimlico in 1938. Aboard is George Woolf, known as "The Iceman" because of his coolness in competition. Seabiscuit's career later was the subject of a motion picture.
Courtesy *The Blood-Horse.*

Kentucky Derby was won by Behave Yourself. With time, this became significant as the first of four Derbys won by Colonel E. R. Bradley. A professional gambler who owned casinos in Palm Beach and Saratoga, Colonel Bradley was advised by his physician to alter his lifestyle. To the degree his constitution made this possible, he became something of a country gentleman, but one more given to sharkskin than tweed.

Colonel Bradley's Idle Hour Stock Farm later raced Derby winners Bubbling Over and Burgoo King. Then, in 1933, he won again. His Brokers Tip battled to the wire with Head Play while their riders battled each other with elbow and whip. Ironically, Bimelech might have been the best horse Bradley bred but he was upset in the 1940 Derby by

Gallahadion. The winner wore the silks of Mrs. Ethel V. Mars, whose Milky Way Stable, was named after her family's famous candy bar.

Colonel Bradley died in 1946, but his significance was extended. The sale of his stock dispersed the blood of the sterling French mare La Troienne, while portions of his land would become the Kentucky division of King Ranch as well as Darby Dan Farm.

The dominant breeder of the 1920s, however, was Harry Payne Whitney, who competed for top honors from 1923 to 1925 with John E. Madden. (The latter had brought Whitney into the game in 1902 when he sold him the crack colt Irish Lad.) Whitney then took over the breeders' list on his own. He or his estate led the list from 1926 through 1932, and

ABOVE

Colonel E. R. Bradley, aided by Kentucky farm manager Olin Gentry, established a sound broodmare band that, after his death, was divided among top-class farms. Thus, the blood of Bradley horses contributed over the years to the success of King Ranch, Greentree Stable, and Ogden Phipps. Horsemen who later bought into the old Bradley families included Hirsch Jacobs, who eventually became a leading breeder. Photograph by Bert Morgan. Courtesy *The Blood-Horse*.

then for two years he and son Cornelius Vanderbilt Whitney were the leaders. Harry Payne Whitney bred 192 stakes winners, a record that lasted until E. P. Taylor of Canada surpassed the mark in 1977. The acquisition of "Whitney mares" was long believed to be the most certain route to success in racing.

Equipoise, nicknamed the Chocolate Soldier, was one of the greatest horses in the Whitney stable. Ten days before H. P. Whitney's death, Equipoise had engaged in a furious tussle with Twenty Grand in the Kentucky Jockey Club Stakes. Twenty Grand was owned by Greentree Stable, launched by the wife of Harry Payne Whitney's brother, Payne Whitney. (The family really liked the name Payne.)

Twenty Grand won in Kentucky, but after H. P. Whitney's death, in the

first big race C. V. "Sonny" Whitney saw as an owner, Equipoise reversed the result. The victory came in the Pimlico Futurity, after which the winning jockey Sonny Workman commented: "It may have been the greatest race anybody ever saw."

Despite his shelly feet, Equipoise raced on through the age of seven, winning 29 of 51 starts. To this day, horsemen of an age to have seen him have a reverence for the Chocolate Soldier, a tribute to his courage as much as to his vaunted speed.

C. V. Whitney did indeed live up to the traditions of his family. Before his death in 1992, he had bred 176 stakes winners, including Counterpoint and Silver Spoon, and had imported the Epsom Derby winner Mahmoud to stand at stud.

One of the men who encour-

ABOVE
The dark little War Admiral was physically different from his big, chestnut sire, Man o' War, but he generally was regarded as Big Red's best son.
War Admiral won the Triple Crown in 1937. He later led the lists both of sires and broodmare sires. Courtesy *The Blood-Horse*.

aged C. V. Whitney to enter racing was William Woodward, Sr. Woodward owned the Belair estate in Maryland, founded by Governor Ogle in the eighteenth century. He bred in the name of Belair Stud, but he had his mares boarded and foals born at Arthur Hancock, Sr.'s, Claiborne Farm in Kentucky. Hancock had expanded his family's historic breeding operation at Ellerslie Stud in Virginia and for a time the Hancocks ran both farms. At Claiborne, Hancock collected a superb band of stallions, and he was the leading breeder four times in the latter 1930s. Woodward was among the investors with Claiborne, as were Warren Wright, Sr., and Mrs. Marion du Pont Scott, who assisted Hancock in importing Sir Gallahad III and Epsom Derby winner Blenheim II. In later years, Hancock's son, A. B. (Bull) Hancock, Jr., imported Nasrullah and secured the services of Princequillo and Bold Ruler. Later came Nijinsky II and then Secretariat, the latter brought in by Bull Hancock's son, Seth. In more recent years, Seth Hancock has maintained the momentum, standing Danzig, Mr. Prospector, Easy Goer, and other major stallions.

William Woodward, Sr.'s, Gallant Fox was trained by Sunny Jim Fitzsimmons, and he won 9 of his 10 races at three in 1930. His lone defeat was a storied one, a race witnessed by Franklin D. Roosevelt as governor of New York. (Franklin, Jr., later owned a Thoroughbred farm in upstate New York.) Belair's Gallant Fox and H. P. Whitney's Whichone were the stars of the year's three year olds, but after a quick deluge so typical of Saratoga in the summer, a 100–1 shot with the stylish name of Jim Dandy splashed home ahead of both. Sent to stud at Claiborne, Gallant Fox quickly begot his own successor as Triple Crown winner in Omaha.

From Florida to Kentucky to New England to Canada to California, the 1920s and 1930s brought new or revived racing.

One of the most spectacular of the new venues was Dr. Charles Strub's grandiose track at Santa Anita, with the craggy San Gabriel Mountains as a backdrop. The California track occupies land adjacent to the original Santa Anita Park, where Lucky Baldwin held races early in the century. Baldwin, who fought Indians during a wagon train crossing from the Midwest to California in the 1850s, made such a fortune in mine speculation, hotels, and canal transport, that he once owned 80,000 acres—known as Rancho Santa Anita then, and downtown Los Angeles today. Late in the nineteenth century, Baldwin had been a regular visitor to Chicago, and raced four winners of the American Derby.

The second coming of Santa Anita was boosted by Dr. Strub's promise of a $100,000 race in 1935.

Such purses were rare at the time. The first Santa Anita Handicap lured crack runners from the top eastern owners including the Whitneys and Alfred Vanderbilt, but Equipoise, Twenty Grand, and Discovery were all defeated by Azucar.

The race, and western racing in general, received a boost from the great horse, Seabiscuit. In the 1920s, Harry Payne Whitney had encouraged Mrs. Henry Carnegie Phipps and her brother, Ogden Mills, to get into racing. Mrs. Phipps founded Wheatley Stable and her heirs are prominent in racing to this day. Among the castoffs of her stable was Seabiscuit, a horse Sunny Jim Fitzsimmons, her trainer, gave 35 starts at two and 12 more at three before selling him off to Charles S. Howard.

ABOVE

An astounding moment in the history of the Kentucky Derby saw Don Meade on winner Brokers Tip (right) scuffle with Herb Fisher on Head Play in the 1933 running. Louisville *Courier-Journal* photographer Wallace Lowry was lying under the rail and caught the moment of a fight that was continued later in the jockeys' room. Courtesy *The Blood-Horse*.

By 1938, Seabiscuit was the star of the West, while the previous season's Triple Crown winner, War Admiral, was the prince of the East. A meeting at Pimlico was arranged by young Alfred Vanderbilt, who then headed that racetrack. Under George Woolf, Seabiscuit took the lead at once and whipped War Admiral.

After repeated losses in the Santa Anita Handicap, the beloved Seabiscuit finally won it at the age of seven in 1940, and became the first horse to exceed $400,000 in earnings. (On the distaff front, a record of unusual longevity had finally fallen when hardy Princess Doreen earned $174,745. Yet another champion bred by John E. Madden, Audley Farm's Princess Doreen, won 34 of 94 starts from 1923–1928.)

Alfred Vanderbilt, who staged the Seabiscuit–War Admiral meeting, also raced one of the stars of the 1930s. In Discovery, Vanderbilt had a perfect example of the modern handicap horse; although he could not defeat Brookmeade Stable's Cavalcade at three, Discovery toured America, stopping at a number of new tracks in New England and the Midwest as well as the traditional circuits of the East. Like Exterminator and very few others, Discovery was a great and consistent weight carrier, carrying as much as 136 pounds successfully.

The 1930s are also important because of the innovations enacted then. Saliva testing reduced the doping of horses, and the identification of racehorses was made easier by the lip tattoo. Starting gates replaced web barriers, pari-mutuels began to replace bookmakers, and public address systems were created so fans could actually hear a race being called. The growth of the racing commission system in each state eroded the central authority of The Jockey Club, but all states looked to The Jockey Club's breeding registry as the official means of qualifying horses to race.

In Florida, Joe Widener built the track at Hialeah and the racing season in the East was expanded into the winter.

AT RIGHT
With architecture reminiscent of a French chateau, and abundant tropical flora, Hialeah became a mecca of sport, society, and fashion.
The 1930s saw War Admiral, and the next decades would bring Whirlaway, Citation, and Nashua. Photograph by Bert Clark Thayer. Courtesy Keeneland-Thayer.

1 9 4 0 – 1 9 6 0

As early as 1934, Calumet Farm, which Warren Wright, Sr., had converted from his father's Standardbred operation, had raced its first Thoroughbred champion, Nellie Flag. Then, in 1939, Wright won the Widener Handicap at Hialeah with his bargain yearling, Bull Lea. As the next decade dawned, Wright hired Ben A. Jones as Calumet's private trainer, and the stately Bluegrass farm had in place a team ready for history.

Wright was also an investor in Blenheim II, the imported Epsom Derby winner and the sire of Calumet's Whirlaway, a fast two year old with a bad habit of sweeping wide toward the outside rail when entering the home

AT LEFT

Saratoga has an aura which has enchanted horse owners and horseplayers for well over a century. The scene here is of a barn beside the training track, known as Oklahoma, on, "Oh, what a beautiful morning." Painting by Elmore Brown. Courtesy Mrs. Walter M. Jeffords, Jr.

stretch. Whirlaway was two for four in Florida during the winter of 1940–1941. For the Kentucky Derby of 1941, Jones had the wisdom to choose Eddie Arcaro, the superstar of then-current jockeys, for his difficult colt. Aided by blinkers that impaired Whirlaway's ability to see to his right, Arcaro brought the colt bursting through the pack to win the Derby by eight lengths in the record time of 2:01⅖. The mark stood for twenty-one years. Whirlaway went on to win the Triple Crown.

Whirlaway was just the beginning for Calumet. As the progeny of Bull Lea began to come to the races, crop after crop had a new champion—Twilight Tear, Armed, Bewitch,

Coaltown, and Two Lea. Best of all was Citation; with Arcaro aboard, he cruised through his and Calumet's second Triple Crown, in 1948. Even when facing older horses early in the year, Citation was their master. He could outsprint the fastest, outstay the stoutest, and do it all with a mechanical rhythm invested of perfection.

Calumet changed coasts in the winter during Citation's career, and his later racing was in California. He raced at Tanforan and Golden Gate in San Francisco as well as Santa Anita and Hollywood Park in Southern California.

After the ankle ailment known as osselets cancelled his entire four-year-old sea-

AT LEFT
Citation convinced Calumet Farm trainer Ben A. Jones that he was the best horse Jones, or anyone else, had ever trained.
He was the first horse after Man o' War to summon frequent comparisons to the earlier champion. Painting by Richard Stone Reeves.
ABOVE
Trainer Jones was aided in the preparation of Whirlaway by Pinky Brown, who exercised champions for Calumet for many years.
Photograph by C. C. Cook. Courtesy Keeneland-Cook.

son, he came back at five, no longer a champion, but still good. The Irish Noor, upstart harbinger of the Nasrullah era in pedigrees, defeated him four times, but Citation was good enough at six to win the 1951 Hollywood Gold Cup. Wright had died several months before, so he did not see the great horse achieve the goal of becoming the first million-dollar earner.

Wright's widow, Lucille, later married Hollywood writer and raconteur Admiral Gene Markey and continued the stable. Measures of Calumet's dominance were many: a record eight Derby winners (including seven from 1941 through 1958), thirteen times the leading breeder in the two decades (eleven consecutive), eleven times the leading owner,

and six Horse of the Year titles in the 1940s. During one summer, in 1952, Jones once saddled fifteen consecutive stakes winners in his division.

Although Calumet dominated the 1940s, other stables were not totally shut out. In 1942, Mr. and Mrs. John D. Hertz's Count Fleet was so spectacular at two in winning the Champagne Stakes and Pimlico Futurity that noted handicapper John B. Campbell assigned him 132 pounds in The Jockey Club's Experimental Free Handicap. The Handicap had been created in the 1930s and continues today, but no horse ever has been assigned a weight to match Count Fleet's. The following spring, with John Longden aboard, Count Fleet toured

ABOVE
Robert J. Kleberg, Jr. (right), established a Kentucky division of King Ranch, but he bred and raised Assault on the vast original spread in Texas.
Trained by Max Hirsch, Assault won the Triple Crown in 1946. Courtesy Helen Alexander/ Middlebrook Farm.

AT RIGHT
Capot carried the salmon-pink and black silks of Greentree Stable. Established by Mrs. Payne Whitney, Greentree later was operated by her children and continues in the 1990s under ownership of Mrs. John Hay Whitney. Capot won the Preakness and Belmont in 1949. Painting by Franklin B. Voss. Courtesy Mrs. John Hay Whitney.

unchallenged through a Triple Crown punctuated with a twenty-five-length victory in the Belmont Stakes. He also threw in a victory in the Withers, completing a foursome that only he and Sir Barton have achieved.

In 1946, Assault won the Triple Crown for the King Ranch. The masterful horseman, cattleman, and oilman Robert J. Kleberg, Jr., bred the colt in Texas, although he also had established a major farm in Kentucky. Assault was injured as a weanling and had an odd, ambling way of walking, but at full speed he was a colt of enduring courage and class. With old Max Hirsch training, he came back as a top-class weight carrier, battling the likes of Stymie, Armed, and the grand mare Gallorette.

Max Hirsch was the breeder of record of the King Ranch's Stymie, a horse that went down in history as one of the great claims. Hirsch Jacobs of New York and his partner, the flamboyant Broadway character Isidor Bieber, claimed Stymie for only $1,500. After being

ABOVE
In the spring and summer of 1952, Native Dancer and jockey Eric Guerin began a heady string of vaulting stretch runs and trips to the winner's circle.
Like Man o' War, Native Dancer was to lose but once in his career; that defeat came in the Kentucky Derby. Photograph by Bert Morgan. Courtesy *The Blood-Horse*.

trained by Jacobs, Stymie won race after race, always charging from behind and earned more than $900,000. In the 1960s, Bieber-Jacobs spent four consecutive years as the leading breeder in earnings in North America, and their homebred champions included Hail to Reason, Affectionately, and Personality. Jacobs trained them all. Hail to Reason sired a winner of each American Triple Crown race as well as Roberto, winner of the prized Epsom Derby.

The most obvious impacts of World War II on racing were inconveniences created by the restriction of gasoline and rubber. Various race meetings were shifted to other tracks, and some racetracks were taken over as training grounds. The racing industry raised some $8.5 million for the War Relief effort, but early in 1945, something about the image of people going to the races offended Washington more than crowds at baseball games. On January 3, James Byrnes, then Director of

ABOVE
Greentree Stable's Tom Fool was a year older than Native Dancer. Their owners were game for a meeting, but injury scuttled the hope for a dream race. Tom Fool went through the 1953 season unbeaten in ten races. Courtesy *The Blood-Horse*.

War Mobilization, ordered the halt of Thoroughbred racing. The lapse was brief, lasting only until May 9, the day after President Truman declared V-E Day.

The champion of 1945 was Busher, a filly bred by Colonel Bradley and later sold to Hollywood mogul Louis B. Mayer of MGM. Mayer's stable grew too vast for his enjoyment, and he undertook a series of dispersals, handled by venerable Humphrey Finney of Fasig-Tipton Company. The Mayer dispersals grossed nearly $4.5 million for 248 horses. Busher was sold to the emerging Maine Chance stable of cosmetics-queen Elizabeth Arden Graham.

The Mayer dispersal also created a new method of syndication. Whereas syndicates in the past had tended to involve four or five investors, Leslie Combs II, owner of Spendthrift Farm in Kentucky, initiated syndicates of some forty shares, with each share entitling the owner to breed one mare per year. On that plan, Combs purchased Beau Pere from Mayer. Undeterred by the stallion's death soon thereafter, Combs also syndicated the unraced Alibhai, destined to be a major stallion. In 1955, the champion Nashua was offered by sealed bid, and Combs had a syndicate together to make Nashua the first horse sold for more than $1 million. The age of syndication had begun in earnest, and briefly in the 1980s would reach such heights that a share, not a whole horse, might be sold for $1 million.

Combs was also the master of the Keeneland yearling sale for many years. The sales division at Keeneland also grew from wartime seeds. In 1943, Fasig-Tipton shifted its traditional Saratoga yearling sale to Lexington because of the difficulty in transporting yearlings, and the success of a "local" sale prompted

ABOVE

Ogden Phipps had his first good horse in the 1930s and has consistently bred and raced outstanding runners in the succeeding decades. These include Buckpasser, Queen of the Stage, Vitriolic, Personal Ensign, and Easy Goer. He also served as chairman of The Jockey Club. Photo by Dell Hancock.

Kentuckians to form Breeders' Sales. In 1945, the average yearling priced leapt above $5,000, whereas it had been under $650 three years earlier. The Breeders' Sales later became the sales division of Keeneland Association, whose July yearling auction eventually became the premier horse sale in the world.

The racetrack at Keeneland had been created in the 1930s by Hal Price Headley and other sportsmen and businessmen and breeders (Headley was all three). It filled a void left in Lexington when the Kentucky Association Track closed after more than 100 years of racing. Keeneland immediately became a jewel within the sport. Hialeah in her glory days saw Winston Churchill and the Duke and Duchess of Windsor, but Keeneland once was visited by the Queen herself.

By the midpoint of the century, Thoroughbred racing had grown enormously: 22,000 starters, a foal crop topping 9,000, and $50 million in purse distribution.

ABOVE
Wheatley Stable's Bold Ruler (right) edged Ralph Lowe's Gallant Man in the 1957 Wood Memorial. Along with Round Table, they made up one of the most memorable trios of three year olds ever seen in a single season. Photograph by Mike Sirico. Courtesy New York Racing Association.

The conduct of racing was different too. Jule Fink won a court case that lessened the authority of The Jockey Club in many matters. In 1950, George D. Widener of Philadelphia was elected chairman of The Jockey Club. In 1962, Widener realized a lifelong ambition by winning the Belmont Stakes, with Jaipur.

The Thoroughbred Racing Associations, an organization of racetracks, grew out of the wartime American Turf Congress. The TRA initiated a security arm, the Thoroughbred Racing Protective Bureau, which has been instrumental in protecting the clean conduct of the sport. Another organization, the Horsemen's Benevolent and Protective Association, took on new importance. Originally intended only for benevolence for man and horse, the national HBPA and its various state divisions became the representatives of owners in negotiations with racetracks over the percentages of the betting handle earmarked for purses. In a sense, the modern HBPA took on one role played by Belmont and James R. Keene at the birth of The Jockey Club.

In the 1930s, Alfred Vanderbilt had gained notoriety as an owner after he purchased Discovery from Mereworth Farm. He also ran Pimlico racetrack, and later became president of Belmont Park, and the chairman of the New York Racing Association. In 1952 Native Dancer, Vanderbilt's homebred son of 1945 Preakness winner Polynesian, became American racing's first televi-

AT LEFT

More than a half-century after riding against Tod Sloan as a young lad, trainer Max Hirsch was congratulated as he led in Middleground following the 1950 Kentucky Derby. The young lad of that moment was Bill Boland, an apprentice at the time. Photography by Skeets Meadors. Courtesy *The Blood-Horse*.

ABOVE

Trainer J. W. Healy was interviewed by Bryan Field after Woof Woof won the Flamingo Stakes at Hialeah in 1940. Track owner J. E. Widener had changed the name of the race from the Florida Derby because he was tired of the word "Derby" being affixed to so many races. A flamingo colony in the infield became part of Hialeah's image. Photograph by Turf Pix. Courtesy Mrs. John Hay Whitney.

sion idol, with his dramatic charges from far back. He swept unbeaten through a two-year-old's campaign of nine races in 1952. The "gray ghost" was still unbeaten at three before failing to catch Dark Star in one of the most dramatic of Kentucky Derby upsets. Native Dancer never lost again, winning the Preakness, Belmont, American Derby, Travers, and many other important races. He was Horse of the Year at four and was retired to Vanderbilt's rambling Sagamore Farm in Maryland to commence a stud career of worldwide influence. Like Man o' War, he had lost but once, winning twenty-one of twenty-two races.

A dream race that never came off was a meeting of Native Dancer and Tom Fool. The latter was bred by Duval Headley and was bought by Greentree Stud, where John Hay Whitney and Joan Whitney Payson had taken over after the death of their mother, Mrs. Payne Whitney. Whitney, who escaped imprisonment in the war by jumping off a train, later owned the New York *Herald-Tribune*; Mrs. Payson owned the New York Mets. Thus, they influenced the life and times of New York City in a variety of ways.

In Tom Fool, Greentree and trainer John Gaver had one of the remarkable runners of his era. A champion at two, a nice colt at three, Tom Fool emerged for an unbeaten season as a handicapper, winning ten of ten in 1953. He carried 136 pounds the day he won the Brooklyn Handicap. The Brooklyn, along with the Metropolitan and Suburban handicaps, long had been recognized as the New York Handicap Triple Crown. Before Tom Fool's sweep of them, only Harry Payne Whitney's Whisk Broom II had won the three races in one year, and that was in 1913.

Continuing a string of extraordinary runners, Nashua and Swaps emerged in the foal crop of 1952 (the

ABOVE

The lot of the jockey is not always glamorous, but neither rain nor mud often stays them from their appointed rounds. Photograph by Morris Gordon. Courtesy Culver Pictures.

AT RIGHT

Horse racing enjoyed a boom after World War II, as well-dressed crowds strained for a glimpse of dusty stretch runs. Courtesy Culver Pictures.

same year the unbeaten Ribot was foaled abroad). Their contrasts created great television drama: Nashua, the willful champion from fashionable Belair Stud; Swaps, the westerner owned by cowboy rancher Rex Ellsworth, who once had driven to Lexington in a pick-up to buy mares but also had negotiated with the Aga Khan to buy the colt's sire, Khaled. Swaps was trained by another cowboy, Mesh Tenney.

After Swaps and Willie Shoemaker turned back Nashua and Eddie Arcaro in the Derby, Swaps returned to the West while Nashua stayed in the East. The public longed for a rematch. Nashua got as far west as Chicago to win the Arlington Classic, and Swaps got as far east as Chicago to win the American Derby. Ben Lindheimer, owner of two Chicago tracks, arranged a match race. National television was on hand as Nashua dashed to the front and never was headed in their $100,000, winner-take-all match race. The race was high in drama, but not in conclusiveness, for Swaps was said to have been unsound beforehand.

From the Kentucky foal crop of 1954 came Bold Ruler and Round Table, joined by the imported Gallant Man. Each had marvelous powers: Bold Ruler was precocious from the start; Round Table campaigned from coast to coast for four years, winning forty-three of sixty-six races and becoming one of the first great grass-course champions; Gallant Man won the Belmont in record time. Each became significant stallions, with Bold Ruler the best, as he topped the sire list eight times.

Bold Ruler was bred and raced by the Wheatley Stable of Mrs. Henry Carnegie Phipps. Mrs. Phipps's sister went abroad and married Lord Granard.

ABOVE

Dancer and actor Fred Astaire, a longtime racing fan and horse owner, hoofed to the winner's circle to receive the trophy after his Triplicate won the Hollywood Gold Cup in 1946. Courtesy *The Blood-Horse*.

In the 1960s, the twin sisters had matching champions named Bold Lad, both by Bold Ruler. Mrs. Phipps's son and grandson became chairmen of The Jockey Club.

The aforementioned Gallant Man was Bill Shoemaker's partner in a unique bit of history. In one race, the great rider mistook the sixteenth pole for the finish line, stood up momentarily, and Gallant Man's bid fell short by a nose. The incident might have been short-lived, but for the moment coming in the Kentucky Derby of all races. The winner was Calumet Farm's Iron Liege, ridden with typical determination by another great rider, Bill Hartack, who matched Eddie Arcaro's record of five Derby wins. Lending yet more drama to the moment was Iron Liege's status as backup to Calumet's General Duke, a colt of exceptional potential, but withdrawn because of injury on Derby eve.

New York's position as a leader in rac-

ing had never seemed vulnerable and had therefore not been consciously protected. By 1953, however, it was deteriorating. That summer, Ogden Phipps, as vice-chairman of The Jockey Club, appointed three distinguished turfmen and American industrialists to develop a plan for New York's revival. They were Captain Harry F. Guggenheim, Christopher T. Chenery, and John W. Hanes.

Guggenheim, Chenery, and Hanes developed a plan to buy the existing tracks in New York City and at Saratoga, where Skiddy von Stade had protected the traditions of the old Spa track. With the help of legislation approved by Averell Harriman, a former racing man who then was governor of New York, the three engineered the formation of the New York Racing Association.

One of the immediate projects was the building of a modern, $33-million

ABOVE

Walter M. Jeffords, Sr., led in Pavot and Eddie Arcaro after the 1945 Belmont Stakes. Jeffords was named an Exemplar of Racing by the National Museum of Racing, and his son followed him into racing. His daughter-in-law remains prominent in the sport. Photograph by Bert Morgan. Courtesy Mrs. Walter M. Jeffords, Jr.

track at Aqueduct. The new track, the Big A, opened in 1959; Guggenheim attempted to win its first feature, the Aqueduct Handicap, with Bald Eagle, but the Cain Hoy colt was second to the Indiana-bred handicap horse Hillsdale.

Before the Big A's first meeting was concluded, Sword Dancer enhanced his successful 1959 Horse of the Year bid by edging Hillsdale and Round Table in a searing edition of the Woodward Stakes. Sword Dancer was among many major runners to fly the colors of Mrs. Isabel Dodge Sloane's Brookmeade Stable, winner of the Kentucky Derby in 1934 with Cavalcade. Sword Dancer's trainer was Elliott Burch, who had succeeded his father, Preston Burch, at the Brookmeade post. Both Burches, along with Preston's father, W. P. Burch, were elected to the Hall of Fame. (The National Museum of Racing and Hall of Fame at Saratoga was dedicated by Governor Harriman in 1955.)

ABOVE

The long history of breeding and racing in Maryland was given further distinction by the hardy mare Gallorette. She frequently faced the best males of the 1940s and here defeats the popular Stymie in the 1946 Brooklyn Handicap. Photograph by Bert Morgan. Courtesy *The Blood-Horse.*

AT RIGHT

Greentree Stable's Shut Out, a son of Equipoise, won the 1942 Kentucky Derby and Travers, trained by John Gaver. More than a half-century elapsed before Sea Hero duplicated that double, in 1993. Painting by Franklin B. Voss. Courtesy Mrs. John Hay Whitney.

1 9 6 0 – 1 9 8 0

The great gelding Kelso's career was a masterpiece, for he passed from upstart three year old into mature champion and finally into grand old warrior. He was Horse of the Year five times consecutively, from 1960 through 1964, from three through seven. He was a horse of steel and heart, and he stole the hearts of those who saw him.

Kelso was bred and raced by Mrs. Richard C. du Pont, was trained most of his career by Carl Hanford, and was ridden through great phases by Eddie Arcaro and Milo Valenzuela. The Master, Arcaro, retired after Kelso's four-year-old season, 1961. That year, Kelso won the New York Handicap Triple

AT LEFT

Richard Stone Reeves for some years portrayed the Horse of the Year for the *Daily Racing Form*. Kelso earned that recognition five times, so he and Reeves grew well acquainted. Jockey Milo Valenzuela was Kelso's regular rider during the final years of the horse's career. Painting by Richard Stone Reeves. Courtesy John D. Schapiro.

Crown. Like Tom Fool, Kelso concluded this series under 136 pounds in the Brooklyn.

Over the seasons, Kelso faced a recurrent wave of younger horses. Eventually, he mastered them, although these were noble runners to be sure, horses such as the popular Carry Back, Crimson Satan, Never Bend, Quadrangle, Gun Bow, Beau Purple, Roman Brother, Ridan, and Jaipur. (In one of the era's famous moments, Jaipur and Ridan ran together virtually throughout the Travers Stakes in Saratoga, Jaipur winning in a photo finish.)

Kelso won thirty-nine of sixty-three races and earned $1,977,896, then a world record. He had a special affinity for The Jockey Club Gold Cup, then raced at two miles, which he won five years in succession. Conversely, the Washington, D.C.,

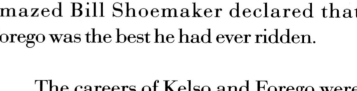

International on grass at Laurel gave him problems: He was beaten every year for three seasons. After the second loss, Valenzuela declared in the jockeys' room: "No horse ever tried like he tried today. Not ever!"

Sweet victory, though, was the ultimate destiny of Kelso. Finally, in 1964, the aging legs carried him past Gun Bow to win the International in a world-record 2:23 ⅖ for 1½ miles on grass.

Another fabulous gelding raced in the following decade was Mrs. Martha Gerry's gigantic Forego. Horse of the Year three times, Forego was so gallant in running down Honest Pleasure to win the 1976 Marlboro Cup under 137 pounds that an amazed Bill Shoemaker declared that Forego was the best he had ever ridden.

The careers of Kelso and Forego were

ABOVE

C. V. Whitney was prominent in racing from 1930 until shortly before his death in 1992. His wife, Marylou Whitney, has kept the name of Whitney deeply involved with racing, with horses tracing to the old Whitney broodmare families. Courtesy New York Racing Association.

AT RIGHT

Horsemen of one generation are apt to bemoan the lessening of challenges of the next era's best horses. In the case of Forego, however, even the staunchest advocates of "the old days" were satisfied. Forego is shown here following one of his four consecutive victories in the Woodward. Photograph by Jerry Cooke.

centered by and large in New York. Old Belmont Park was condemned in the early 1960s, but the NYRA decided to renovate it. The grand lady of the turf was reopened in 1968 in time for an auspicious occasion—the 100th running of the Belmont Stakes. Fittingly, one of the historic stables, Greentree, won that Belmont, with Stage Door Johnny.

A large part in the building of these tracks was played by John W. Galbreath, who had made a fortune in real estate and development in his native Columbus, Ohio. Galbreath launched his Darby Dan Farm in the 1930s and later converted part of Colonel E. R. Bradley's Idle Hour Stock Farm in Lexington into the Kentucky division of Darby Dan. He bought the best and he got results. It was Galbreath who stood Swaps after purchasing him in two $1-million halves, and Galbreath, too, who secured the great Ribot and

Sea-Bird II from Europe via seven-figure leases.

Darby Dan, still run by John W. Galbreath's family, won the Kentucky Derby and Belmont with Chateaugay in 1963 and the Derby with Proud Clarion in 1967. In 1972 Galbreath's homebred Roberto carried his silks to victory in the Epsom Derby. Even so, his most spectacular colt was Graustark, a sensation in every race but was forced to the sidelines in the weeks before the Kentucky Derby in 1966.

Galbreath's Roberto was part of a trend of the 1960s and 1970s that had ramifications in the markets of the world as well as on the racecourses. This trend reversed a pattern of some 2½ centuries, which presumed that England was the test source of high-quality Thoroughbreds. Americans had bred some great racehorses as well, and U.S. Ambassador to

ABOVE
During late Victorian and early Edwardian times, English owners sought to honor their horses' memories by having a hoof made into an inkwell.
A more graceful form of respect is the grave and tombstone. Secretariat was buried with honors at Claiborne Farm after his death at nineteen. Photograph by Dell Hancock.

AT RIGHT
In an era of Vietnam and Watergate, Secretariat had taken on a comforting role in America, reminding that, once in awhile,
excellence and beauty could still be an uplifting aspect of life. Painting by Richard Stone Reeves. Courtesy National Museum of Racing.

Ireland Raymond Guest was one of those who proved it. Guest was a cousin of Winston Churchill and once jotted impromptu notes on the NATO alliance on toilet paper at Chequers. He won the Epsom Derby and Laurel International in 1968 with the noble American colt Sir Ivor.

No American-bred had won the grand Epsom event since Robert Sterling Clark's Never Say Die (jockey Lester Piggott's first Derby winner) in 1954. Quickly, however, North American success became a trend. Sir Ivor was followed two years later by Canadian-bred Nijinsky II, England's first Triple Crown winner since Bahram thirty-five years before. Then came Paul Mellon's Virginia-bred Mill Reef to win the 1971 Derby, and add France's Prix de l'Arc de Triomphe, the climactic event of the European season. Roberto came along the next year, to be followed by other North American-bred Derby winners includ-

ing Empery, The Minstrel, and Henbit.

The world took notice of such horses and beat a path to the doors of American breeders, specifically at the four most important yearling sales: Fasig-Tipton Kentucky and Keeneland in July, Saratoga in August, and Keeneland again in September. At the beginning of the 1960s, platinum-magnate Charles Engelhard had bought a number of horses for sale-topping prices in the $100,000 range, spectacular at the time. Nijinsky II, Ribocco, and Ribero were among North American yearlings the ponderous mogul bought here and won classics with abroad.

Englishman Robert Sangster and his various partners were among those who raised the ante higher and higher until yearlings were selling for more than $1 million. Sangster, along with Stavros Niarchos made it pay, with horses such as The Minstrel, Golden Fleece, and Nureyev.

ABOVE

Northern Dancer was small enough that a special elevation had to be arranged for him to cover mares in his first season at stud. Yet his profound influence on the breed continues some thirty years after the Canadian's initial fame as a classic winner. Photograph by The Drummer Boy. Courtesy *The Blood-Horse*.

Much of this had to do with a little colt named Northern Dancer, with which Canada's E. P. Taylor had proven that good horses could be raised in Ontario. Northern Dancer won the Kentucky Derby and Preakness and his own country's unique Queen's Plate. He stood at Taylor's Windfields Farm in Canada and later at the Maryland division of Windfields. Northern Dancer quickly began compiling the record that would place him among the great stallions of any century, and three of his sons (Nijinsky II, The Minstrel, and Secreto) won the Epsom Derby. Nijinsky II in turn sired two more Derby winners, Golden Fleece and Shahrastani, and other sons have already sired more Derby winners. Lyphard, Nureyev, and Danzig are others among Northern Dancer's distinguished sons at stud today.

Taylor passed Harry Payne Whitney as the all-time leading breeder of stakes winners in 1977, with 193. By the time of his death only twelve years later, the dynamic Canadian industrialist and sportsman had raised the total to an astounding 323. He led North American breeders in earnings nine times, at one point alternating at the top with the likes of historic Elmendorf Farm (then owned by Maxwell Gluck) and Claiborne Farm.

Northern Dancer was the second Kentucky Derby winner for his trainer, Horatio Luro. The Argentine-born Luro had won two years earlier with Californian George Pope's Decidedly, the colt that broke Whirlaway's Derby record. Northern Dancer reduced the mark to 2:00. In the 1930s and 1940s, the dashing Señor Luro had brought Argentine horses into this country with telling success, and he had turned the European colt Princequillo from a claimer into a distinguished stayer. Princequillo later was a leading sire.

Before Northern Dancer, there had been Bold Ruler

ABOVE

Ogden Mills Phipps was elected to The Jockey Club in 1965 and became chairman in 1983. His father, Ogden Phipps, is a past chairman, a post which also has been filled by two generations of August Belmonts and former Secretary of the Treasury Nicholas F. Brady. Photograph by Dell Hancock.

standing at Claiborne for Mrs. Phipps's Wheatley Stable. In the early 1960s came the first wave of champions sired by Bold Ruler, including Bold Lad and Queen Empress, champion two-year-old colt and filly in 1964. Two years later came Bold Lad's full brother, Successor, to be juvenile champion, and then Mrs. Phipps's son, Ogden Phipps, took charge of the juvenile division. His colt Vitriolic and filly Queen of the Stage won the titles in 1967, and both were sired by Bold Ruler.

Slipping in amidst the Bold Rulers was Ogden Phipps's Buckpasser. A son of Tom Fool, Buckpasser was a champion at two, three, and four, and he once ran off fifteen consecutive triumphs. He was given to dramatic finishes, such as the 1967 Suburban Handicap, when he appeared beaten by Ring Twice, but vaulted forward to pick up the two lengths he needed in eighty yards. Under 133 pounds, Buckpasser gave Ring Twice twenty-two pounds.

Wheatley twice was the leading owner in the middle

ABOVE
The stretch runs of Carry Back carried him to victory in the Kentucky Derby and Preakness of 1961 and many other triumphs. His owners, Jack and Kathryn Price, had been such fans of the turf as a young couple that they treated as keepsakes the cards on which Saratoga hotels once printed the names of current guests. Photograph by Jerry Cooke.

1960s, and Eddie Neloy, who trained for both Phipps stables, was the leading trainer three times in succession. Not all the Bold Rulers raced for the Phippses, of course. Among other champions by the super sire were Lamb Chop and Gamely, both distaffers raced in the colors of William Haggin Perry. The latter had entered into a partnership with the Hancocks to race Claiborne-bred horses jointly. One of the most enduring of associations, the partnership continued even after the era's predominant breeder, Bull Hancock, died in 1972.

Overlapping Buckpasser's career were the campaigns of Damascus and Dr. Fager. Damascus won by ten lengths when all three met in the 1967 Woodward Stakes, but Dr. Fager lowered Buckpasser's world record for the mile to 1:32⅕. Dr. Fager was a Florida-bred Rough 'n Tumble colt bred and raced by Tartan Farms and trained by John Nerud. Damascus, a Sword Dancer colt, flew the old white silks with red polka dots of Belair Stud; his owner and breeder was Mrs. Thomas Bancroft, a

ABOVE

In 1966, Braulio Baeza teamed with the powerful champion Buckpasser. The rider had suffered a blow earlier that year when Graustark, which he rode under contract for Darby Dan Farm, was injured and forced into retirement. Buckpasser won thirteen of fourteen races that season and was Horse of the Year. Photograph by Jerry Cooke.

daughter of William Woodward, Sr.

Damascus was trained by Frank Whiteley, who also trained Tom Rolfe, Forego, and Ruffian. Mr. and Mrs. Stuart Janney's Ruffian was a wonder filly. She was unbeaten in ten races and was so swift that she was widely expected to defeat Kentucky Derby winner Foolish Pleasure when they lined up for a match race at Belmont Park in 1975. Instead, Ruffian broke down early and valiant veterinary attempts to save her were unsuccessful.

In the late 1960s, racing suffered considerable turmoil, especially over the issue of medicating horses. When Dancer's Image won the Kentucky Derby in 1968, the roses were not even wilted before it was announced that he had tested positive for Butazolidin. After many hear-

ings and court battles, the disqualification upheld, giving Calumet Farm's Forward Pass a tarnished Derby trophy. Soon thereafter, many states recognized Bute as a therapeutic medication, and it is allowed in virtually all jurisdictions, as is Lasix, a protection against exercise-induced pulmonary hemorrhage.

Dancer's Image would have been the second Maryland-bred son of Native Dancer to win the Derby in three years. Kauai King had won the Derby and Preakness in 1966. Maryland's fund for supplementing purses and providing breeders' awards was not the first incentive program for a state's breeders, but its impact was one of the most obvious. The fund helped restore vitality to the breeding industry in the state. Incentive programs were to become so widespread

ABOVE

The world-record holder at a mile, Dr. Fager, was named for the physician who performed brain surgery on trainer John Nerud. Dr. Fager was bred and owned by Tartan Farm and represented the heights for his sire, Rough 'n Tumble. The sire was instrumental in the emergence of Florida as a major Thoroughbred producer. Courtesy *The Blood-Horse.*

AT RIGHT

Vaughn Flannery left the hectic world of Madison Avenue advertising and applied his art to graceful depiction of the charms of Thoroughbreds, farms, and racetracks, including this scene from Belmont Park. Courtesy Mrs. John Hay Whitney.

that by the early 1990s, slightly more than ten percent of all purse monies went for races restricted to runners bred in host programs. The programs also created ongoing debate as to what form they should take to provide proper incentive for improvement rather than merely subsidizing continued foal production.

The late 1960s also saw the development of the Coggin's test to detect the deadly disease known as Swamp Fever. Occasional outbreaks of the disease had haunted the industry since the 1940s. Later, in the 1970s, racing endured an outbreak of Venezuelan equine encephalomyelitis, which was fatal, and then contagious equine metritis. An outbreak of equine viral arteritis would also flare briefly. The latter two prompted specific codes of practice on breeding farms.

In California in 1969, John Longden had his first star as a trainer; it was a colt named Majestic Prince, in the first crop of Raise a Native. In the Keeneland sale ring, Majestic Prince had brought $250,000, then a world

ABOVE

The silks of white, with red polka dots, prominent on the American scene since the days of William Woodward, Sr.'s, Gallant Fox, were flown by a latter-day champion. Damascus, owned by one of Woodward's daughters, Mrs. Thomas Bancroft, was Horse of the Year in 1967. Photograph by Bob Coglianese. Courtesy New York Racing Association.

record for a yearling.

In the Kentucky Derby and Preakness in 1969, Majestic Prince and jockey Bill Hartack battled grimly to the wire ahead of Paul Mellon's Arts and Letters ridden by Braulio Baeza. But Majestic Prince could not keep pace in the stretch of what proved his final race, the Belmont. Arts and Letters, a son of Ribot, won the Belmont and dominated the rest of the season to be Horse of the Year. Mellon's Rokeby Stable was back the following year with Fort Marcy, garnering a share of Horse of the Year honors with Personality.

By the end of the 1971 season, the *Daily Racing Form*, TRA, and the National Turf Writers Association had unified year-end championship balloting by forming the Eclipse Awards. First Horse of the Year under the Eclipse Award plan was Ack Ack, raced in California for actress Greer Garson and trained by Charlie

Whittingham. A one-time partner and running mate of Horatio Luro, Whittingham had been a trainer of prominent horses since he raced Porterhouse for Liz Whitney-Tippett's long-successful Llangollen Stable in 1954. Whittingham, a tall, bald fellow with sprightly step and outlook to match, seems always to have a stable of major runners. He also won two Kentucky Derbys in the 1980s, with Ferdinand and Sunday Silence.

Secretariat, a muscular chestnut by Bold Ruler, was bred by Christopher T. Chenery's Meadow Stud, a prominent stable since Hill Prince swapped classic wins with Middleground in the early 1950s. During the 1960s, Chenery's filly Cicada was a champion at two, three, and four, and his Sir Gaylord would have likely been the Derby favorite of 1962 but for an injury at the eleventh hour. By 1971, when Meadow's Riva Ridge was champion two

ABOVE

Charlie Whittingham once trained a popular old claimer, the stretch-running Malicious. Since the 1950s, his hand has been turned to classier horses, and he has won an extraordinary collection of the best West Coast races as well as Kentucky Derbys with Ferdinand and Sunday Silence. Photograph by Dell Hancock.

year old, Chenery was enfeebled, and a daughter, Helen B. (Penny) Chenery, directed the stable. Riva Ridge came close to a Triple Crown for Meadow, trainer Lucien Laurin, and jockey Ron Turcotte, winning the Derby and Belmont. Secretariat went the whole route.

Secretariat's dominance of two-year-old races was dramatized by his preference for closing ground on the turns, and he was spectacular enough to be voted Horse of the Year as a juvenile. At three, Secretariat raced through the Triple Crown with such flare that he was likened to Man o' War and Citation.

If skyrocketing prices were the anthem of the yearling market of the middle 1970s, bargains were the countermelody. In 1976, the Derby and Belmont were won by Bold Forbes, bought for only $15,200, and the Preakness went to Elocutionist, purchased for $15,000. Both were sold as yearlings at the Fasig-Tipton Kentucky sale. That same year, two young couples, Jim and Sally Hill and Mickey and Karen Taylor, bought a son of Bold

Reasoning for $17,500. They named him Seattle Slew and in 1977 he became the only horse to win the Triple Crown while undefeated. At four, Slew survived a near-fatal illness and returned to the track for a meeting of former Triple Crown winners. Slew ran off from Affirmed in the Marlboro Cup, confirming the old adage that a good older horse will beat a good three year old.

Affirmed was a homebred owned by Louis Wolfson's Harbor View Farm, which had bought his grandsire, Raise a Native, and bred his sire, Exclusive Native. Wolfson had joined the early waves of horsemen to establish major farms in Florida, a group whose ranks also included Fred Hooper and Howard and Tim Sams of Waldemar, Ocala Stud, Hobeau and Tartan farms. Since the late 1950s, he had owned prominent horses, and his Roman Brother succeeded Kelso as Horse of the Year on one year-end poll in 1965.

Affirmed was one partner in the greatest rivalry in American racing. His counterpart was Alydar, another son

ON FOLLOWING PAGE

Paul Mellon frequently led in his grass-course specialist Fort Marcy (Jorge Velasquez aboard). Earlier, Fort Marcy's form on dirt had prompted his entry in a sale, but he was retained when bidding was desultory. Photograph by Bob Coglianese. Courtesy New York Racing Association.

of Raise a Native, owned by Calumet Farm. Alydar was trained by young John Veitch, whose father, Syl, had trained Counterpoint, Phalanx, and First Flight for C. V. Whitney.

In two years, Affirmed defeated Alydar seven times in ten meetings. On the surface this would indicate a basic lack of tension in the air when they met, but with this pair, it was not what they did, but how they did it. Again and again they came to the wire together—only a half-length separated them in the Hopeful, a nose in the Futurity, a neck in the Laurel Futurity, and a neck in the Preakness. Affirmed won all of these. Alydar at other times got in his licks, but Affirmed held sway throughout the Triple Crown.

The climax came in the Belmont. As the daughter of Hirsch Jacobs, Mrs. Wolfson had seen many a stirring struggle in the stretch of the old track, but few races have approached the 1978 Belmont. Teenager Steve Cauthen rode Affirmed along the inside, and Jorge Velasquez steered Alydar on the outside. Affirmed won by a head. Neither seemed defeated.

ON FOLLOWING PAGES

A remarkable duo of triples occurred in the late 1970s, when Seattle Slew (page 148) won the Triple Crown in 1977 and was followed the next year by another Triple Crown winner, Affirmed (page 149). They later squared off in the first meeting of Triple Crown winners. Paintings by Richard Stone Reeves.

Seattle Slew—Courtesy Mr. and Mrs. Mickey Taylor. Affirmed—Private Collection.

AFFIRMED   RICHARD STONE REEVES

THE 1980S AND 1990S

Not since Regret in 1915 had a filly won the Kentucky Derby, but in the spring of 1980 Genuine Risk took the lead near the stretch of Churchill Downs and never relinquished it. Like Regret, she was a chestnut with a white blaze, and she had the nerve and heart to outrun a field of males.

Genuine Risk raced for the prominent stable of Bert and Diana Firestone and followed Foolish Pleasure as the second Derby winner trained by LeRoy Jolley. A $31,500 bargain bred by Mrs. G. Watts Humphrey, Jr., Genuine Risk was even tougher then her Derby showed. She had prepped against males in the Wood Memorial and went right through the Triple Crown,

AT LEFT
Well into its second century, the Kentucky Derby continued its role as a rite of spring.
The advent of simulcasting made the race all the more personal to many Americans. Photograph by Jerry Cooke.

placing behind Codex in the Preakness and Temperence Hill in the Belmont.

The 1980s also marked the final campaign of Spectacular Bid. Yet another in a series of bargain yearlings, the Bold Bidder colt had been purchased by Hawksworth Farm for $37,000 in 1977. He had been champion at two and had waltzed through the Derby and Preakness of 1979 at three, but was beaten by Coastal in the Belmont. In 1980, trainer Bud Delp sent the big colt through a campaign that had all the perfection of Tom Fool's season twenty-seven years before. Spectacular Bid raced nine times from January to September, from 7 furlongs to 1 ¼ miles, in California, Chicago, New Jersey, and New York. He carried 130 pounds or more five times. And he won all nine races. Along the way, he lowered the world record for 1 ¼ miles to 1:57 ⅖.

If Spectacular Bid represented a classic bargain, John Henry took racing's rags-to-riches saga to extremes.

Once sold for a little as $1,100, he knocked around the lesser tracks of Louisiana before he landed in the stable of big-time trainer Ron McAnally. In 1980, John Henry marched through eight wins in twelve starts and was the champion male on grass. At six, he was even better, winning eight of ten, and was Horse of the Year. Among his remarkable triumphs was a victory by a nose over The Bart in the first Arlington Million. In his next start, John Henry moved from grass to dirt and won The Jockey Club Gold Cup. John won two Santa Anita Handicaps, and another Arlington Million during a second Horse of the Year season at the age of nine in 1984. His lifetime earnings of $6,597,947 stood at the time as a world record.

A startling illustration of how far the yearling boom went was the sale of Seattle Slew's half-brother, Seattle Dancer, for double what John Henry earned. During the early 1980s, the Maktoums, the ruling family of oil-rich Dubai, began investing in the bloodstock both here and in Europe at an unprecedented level. They

AT LEFT

John Henry added his legendary name to the list of great, enduring geldings of the past, such as Old Rosebud, Exterminator, Armed, Kelso and Forego. The one-time $1,100 yearling earned more than $6 million. Chris McCarron was among the riders who teamed with him. Photograph by Katey Barrett.

had instant and sustained success more or less commensurate with the millions they anted up to play the game at the top. For Seattle Dancer, however, they were outbid by Robert Sangster's group at $13.1 million.

Seattle Dancer was consigned to the Keeneland July sale of 1985 by two of the prime movers of the industry, Warner L. Jones, Jr., and William S. Farish. Jones owns Hermitage Farm and was chairman of Churchill Downs; Farish owns Lane's End Farm and succeeded Jones at the Derby track. Farish also is vice chairman of The Jockey Club. He had scored his first major triumph when Bee Bee Bee upset Riva Ridge in the Preakness Stakes of 1972.

Seattle Dancer was a stakes winner in Europe, but the earning potential of such investment was geared toward his stud career. He symbolized the height, and the end, of an insupportable spiral. Select yearlings at Keeneland and Saratoga averaged $416,515 in 1985, but less than half that, $193,987, in 1992. Overall, North American yearlings averaged $20,646 at the highest and were averaging $15,924 in 1992.

Ramifications of such spasms in the industry were many. The heady upward spiral encouraged a raft of partnerships, many peopled by investors with little knowledge of or commitment to racing. Most of these partnerships were failures. As the price of horses collapsed, many commercial breeders who had borrowed money to purchase at the top found themselves selling in a declining market. By the early 1990s, some twenty percent of Bluegrass farms were said to be for

ABOVE

Any trainer in the spring of 1980 would have been cautious over running a filly in the Kentucky Derby, since no distaffer had won it in sixty-five years. Owner Bert Firestone (left) thought it worth the effort with Genuine Risk, and trainer LeRoy Jolley (right) prepared the filly for her historic 1980 triumph. Photograph by Dell Hancock.

sale. Still, to those who survived the trauma, the return to a more stable horse market had the potential to be a long-term benefit.

Concomitant with the upheavals in the market came a withering sequence of sellouts. Spendthrift Farm was sold on the courthouse steps early in 1993. But the most dramatic demise was that of storied Calumet Farm. After the death of Mrs. Gene Markey in 1982, a somewhat distant in-law, J. T. Lundy, took over management of the farm. While Lundy turned out such successful runners as Horse of the Year Criminal Type and Kentucky Derby winner Strike the Gold, startling financial woes came to light. Eventually, with debt having risen from zero to some $127 million and with the farm's great stallion Alydar having

died, Calumet was sold at auction to Henryk de Kwiatkowski.

De Kwiatkowski represented one of the era's positive sagas, and his trainer, Woody Stephens, perhaps represented its most amazing success story. Stephens had been a prominent trainer since the 1940s and handled the leading money-winning outfit in America in 1959, as the private trainer for Cain Hoy Stable. In 1974 Stephens had saddled John M. Olin's Cannonade to win the Kentucky Derby, viewed by a record crowd of 163,628. Nothing, however, matched the sequence Stephens commenced with Conquistador Cielo in 1982. That Mr. Prospector colt was the first of five consecutive winners of the Belmont Stakes trained by Stephens. He was followed by Caveat (1983), Swale (1984), Creme Fraiche (1985),

ABOVE

Genuine Risk not only won the Derby but continued along the Triple Crown trail, placing in the Preakness and Belmont. Ill luck plagued her as a broodmare, and she did not have a live foal until 1993. Courtesy New York Racing Association.

and de Kwiatkowski's Danzig Connection (1986).

In 1974 Ogden Phipps had been succeeded as chairman of The Jockey Club by Nicholas F. Brady, whose father, James Cox Brady, had raced a major stable and had been a chairman of the NYRA. When Brady was appointed to complete a term as a United States senator, August Belmont IV succeeded him as The Jockey Club's chairman. (Brady later served as Secretary of the Treasury in the Bush Administration.) Belmont in turn was succeeded in 1983 by Ogden Phipps's son, Ogden Mills Phipps. Like his father and grandmother, the younger Phipps had developed a major stable of his own. Likewise, his sister, Cynthia Phipps, races her own runners, using the old Wheatley Stable colors.

Woody Stephens's 1984 Belmont Stakes winner, Swale, had a place in history too. In all the years of Claiborne Farm's eminence, dating back some seventy years, the farm's goldish orange silks never had been worn to victory in a Kentucky Derby. Bull Hancock and his father died without realizing that dream, but in 1984 Swale achieved what no Claiborne runner had before. After his Derby win, Swale faltered in the Preakness, but came back to win the Belmont. He died suddenly at Stephens's stable the next week of a syndrome never identified.

Bull Hancock's older son, Arthur III, had established his own operation, Stone Farm, some time after his father's death. Two years before Swale's triumph, Arthur had broken through for the family in seeing his colors carried to victory in the Derby by Gato Del Sol, bred and raced in partnership with Leone J. Peters. Seven years later, Arthur Hancock's silks were carried to the roses again by Sunday Silence, owned in partnership with trainer Charlie Whittingham and Dr. Ernest Galliard.

Perhaps contemporary problems tend to appear magnified by their very proximity when, in fact, they are not larger than other eras' problems, merely closer. At any rate, racing in the 1980s and 1990s has seen itself beset by an abundance of worries. In addition to the dynamics of the bloodstock market, the industry for the

AT LEFT

Spectacular Bid won the Kentucky Derby in 1979, and through 1993 remained the last two-year-old champion to come back and win the classic. Spectacular Bid added an unbeaten campaign at four in 1980. Photograph by Kevin Ellsworth. Courtesy Hollywood Park.

first time in many decades faced a decline in foal supply. The foal crop peaked at 51,293 in 1986. The Jockey Club registered a decline totaling twenty-four percent over the next half-dozen years. Traditionalists of most eras have tended to view the growth in foal crops as "overproduction." However, by the 1990s, North American racing offered 8,641 racing days at 133 tracks and 89,724 individual starters annually. Such growth demands mass numbers of foals in order to function. Purse levels had soared to $780 million, but there was indication that the supply of owners was dwindling.

Central to the health of the racing industry, of course, is the amount of pari-mutuel wagering and the amounts derived from it by the racetracks and horsemen (in the form of purses). A long, often demoralizing struggle to convince state legislatures that less tax taken off the top would encourage more activity and a healthier industry was won in small increments. Nevertheless, decreased taxation did not, in fact, blossom into consistent prosperity.

ABOVE
Swale fulfilled a dream harbored by three generations of the Hancock family, when he carried the Claiborne Farm silks to victory in the Kentucky Derby in 1984.
Photograph by Dell Hancock.

The advanced technology of communications has become a prime factor in the structure of the sport. The Ontario Jockey Club experimented with simulcasting races among the tracks it owned in the late 1970s. Soon, simulcasting became the rage, both interstate and intrastate. At the same time, more and more states moved to legalize and establish offtrack-betting networks.

Thus, in fairly short order, the situation changed from a fan having to attend the races in order to bet legally on them to his having a variety of choices—posh Manhattan OTB clubs, or seedier ones in the same city; sports bars for the yuppy, the redneck, or the cruise-ship customer; and fairgrounds and racetracks that took bets from elsewhere when they themselves were dark. Next came the beginnings of tracks taking whole-card signals from elsewhere at the same time they were running their own meetings, as had proven popular in Australia. Telephone-accounting betting had been introduced in several states here, and ahead lay increased use of inter-

ABOVE

Woody Stephens had been a successful trainer for some four decades before he launched an unprecedented string of classic victories winning the Belmont Stakes five years in succession with Conquistador Cielo (1982), Caveat (1983) , Swale (1984), Creme Fraiche (1985), and Danzig Connection (1986). Photograph by Dell Hancock.

active betting machines, ultimately (perhaps) home television units, along with handheld betting terminals for use on- or offtrack.

If racing leaders were tempted to think they were facing more problems than their predecessors, who could blame them?

The good news was that racing leaders were mindful of the need to be planners, rather than always reacting to outside influences. The TRA established its 1995 Committee when 1995 seemed to be far enough in the future for matters still to be shaped. One of the outgrowths of active planning was early development of a National Pick Six, wherein fans around North America could participate in a large pool and watch the races on television. Also, a national plan for betting on the new Breeders' Cup was

developed, a splendid example of cutting through the red tape of multiple jurisdictions for the common advancement of all of them.

The Jockey Club became more and more visible in its service orientation and reached out to include members from various parts of the country, seeking active leaders. In partnership with the TRA, The Jockey Club formed Equibase, a plan designed for the industry to have better control and make better use of its statistics. The Jockey Club also launched a commercial information company, continued its long-established foundation to support disabled industry individuals, helped underwrite Thoroughbred Racing Communications, and continued its Round Table Conferences annually in

AT LEFT

American yearling auctions had been frequent affairs since late in the nineteenth century, but in the 1970s and 1980s they reached such heights that million-dollar prices for yearlings became commonplace. Photograph by Dell Hancock.

ABOVE

By the early 1990s, the yearling market had receded but impressive figures were still required to purchase the best prospects when buyers gathered from around the world for an auction. Photograph by Dell Hancock.

Saratoga. In its role as guarantor of the integrity of the breed registry, The Jockey Club had instituted blood-typing, and by the 1990s had invested in converting to even more certain identity by the use of DNA.

The Jockey Club also merged its own veterinary sciences support element with the Grayson Foundation, which since the 1940s had been a leader in support of equine research. Veterinary science in the last decade accelerated developments, with all manner of improvements, including arthroscopic surgery, lazer surgery, scintigraphy, and increased refinement of electronic pregnancy evaluations. Universities prominent in equine research include Cornell, the University of Pennsylvania (New Bolton Center), the University of Kentucky (Maxwell Gluck Center), Oklahoma State, Kansas State, Washington State, and Florida. Although the American Association of Equine Practitioners is not a Thoroughbred racing organization per se, the AAEP offered increased leadership in matters concerning medication control, sale warranties, and racetrack safety.

Amid the daunting problems and workaday matters, the Breeders' Cup stands out as a monumental advancement in Thoroughbred racing. It was born of the determination of John R. Gaines, who as former owner of Gainesway Farm was one of the breeding industry's prime movers for the last two decades. Gainesway's group of international stallions included Blushing Groom, Vaguely Noble, Lyphard, and Riverman. Gaines later sold the farm to Graham Beck of South Africa.

Gaines saw the Breeders' Cup as an opportunity to provide the sport a championship day and generate positive promotion at the same time. The Cup has accomplished that and more, offering $10 million in purses on the big day itself, which has been televised live since its inception. Moreover, an ancillary program of stakes races and purse supplements, sponsored by Budweiser, has multiplied the number of individual horsemen benefitting from the Breeders' Cup and kept the organization visible throughout the year.

AT LEFT

Winning Colors, in the powerful stable D. Wayne Lukas trained for former San Diego Chargers owner Eugene Klein, won the 1988 Santa Anita Derby under Gary Stevens. That spring, she would become the third filly to win the Kentucky Derby. Courtesy Santa Anita Park.

In less than a decade, the Breeders' Cup has taken its place in the central core of events that motivate and shape the campaigns of the best and the swiftest.

The first Breeders' Cup (financed largely through stallion and foal nominations) was assigned to Hollywood Park, then run by Marje Everett. From the first, the Breeders' Cup has been the dazzling showcase of racing and has been embraced wholeheartedly by Europeans. The first Breeders' Cup Turf was won by Aga Khan's longshot Lashkari. The beaten field included Daniel Wildenstein's singular mare All Along. The previous year, the well-traveled All Along had been voted Horse of the Year over the unbeaten juvenile Devil's Bag; she crossed the Atlantic almost as if on a shuttle, winning the Laurel International, Woodbine's Rothman's International, and Belmont's Turf Classic as well as the Arc at home. Prince Khaled Abdullah was game enough to send his dominant European champion Dancing Brave into the heat of California when the

Cup was staged by the Oak Tree Association at Santa Anita in 1986. The horse was fourth behind Manila, but the sportsmanship of accepting the challenge was in keeping with the aims of the Breeders' Cup.

The first running of the $3 million Breeders' Cup Classic, the richest race in the world, was won by Wild Again in a pulsating duel with the champion Slew o' Gold and Preakness winner Gate Dancer.

When the Cup returned to Hollywood again in 1987, the turf was won by Allen Paulson and Bert Firestone's Theatrical in a dramatic duel with Arc winner Trempolino. A half-hour later, that duel seemed almost mild by comparison to the battle of Kentucky Derby winners that had ennobled the Breeders' Cup Classic. Mrs. Howard Keck's Ferdinand barely edged the Clarence Scharbauer family's current-year Derby winner, Alysheba. The winning rider was Bill Shoemaker, who retired in 1990 with an all-time record 8,833 wins. (He was paralyzed in an auto accident later,

AT RIGHT
Mrs. Jane du Pont Lunger's Go For Wand won the Breeders' Cup Juvenile Fillies at Gulfstream Park in 1989. The following year, she suffered a fatal spill while trying for a second Breeders' Cup triumph. Photograph by Steve Stidham. Courtesy Stidham & Associates.

but struggled back to continue his new career as a trainer, from a wheelchair.)

Alysheba was the top star of a crop that included Bet Twice and Java Gold. One of the many important horses owned over the years by Paul Mellon's Rokeby Stable, Java Gold was forced out of action before the Breeders' Cup. Kentuckian Mack Miller succeeded Elliott Burch as trainer for Mellon, who remained a philanthropist of towering magnitude, in supporting racing art as well as other areas. In 1993, the Mellon-Miller team won the Kentucky Derby with Sea Hero. Later than spring, Mr. Mellon donated $1 million to the Grayson Foundation, which specializes in equine research.

Despite the rapid development of veterinary techniques, tragedy visited the Breeders' Cup in 1990, when Go for Wand, a streaking young filly in the Christiana Stable of Mrs. Jane Lunger, fell abruptly. She could not be saved. Until that convulsive lurch of fortunes, she had been engaged in a stirring duel with the Argentina

mare Bayakoa, winner of the Breeders' Cup Distaff for a second time.

During the 1970s, the Japanese had a phase of high visibility in the world's best bloodstock markets, and by the 1990s they had returned to a similar role, although never to the degree of the Maktoums. This Japanese influence also was reflected in the Breeders' Cup. The 1992 Horse of the Year and Breeders' Cup Classic winner was A. P. Indy, trained by Neil Drysdale through a sequence of hoof problems for owner Tomonora Tsurumaki. A. P. Indy had been the top-priced yearling of 1990, when purchased at Keeneland for $2.9 million from William S. Farish and W. S. Kilroy. He was by Seattle Slew and was a half-brother to Dogwood Stable's 1990 Preakness winner, Summer Squall.

Other occasions when the Breeders' Cup concluded a successful Horse of the Year campaign included the 1989 running at Gulfstream Park. Easy Goer and Sunday Silence had furnished racing one of its historic

AT LEFT

Proof of the impact a racehorse can have was Arazi s stirring triumph in the 1991 Breeders' Cup Juvenile. Allen Paulson's French-raced champion rushed from last to first in his initial race on dirt to become an instant hero and apparent super horse in the making. Photograph by Anne M. Eberhardt. Courtesy *The Blood-Horse*.

moments in the Preakness, battling through the stretch with all the crackle of an Affirmed-Alydar duel. Sunday Silence won by a lip and had also won the Derby, but Easy Goer ran away from him in the Belmont. In their climactic meeting in the Breeders' Cup, the agile Sunday Silence burst into the lead and held off the menacing rush of the other colt.

Lady's Secret clinched Horse of the Year in another manner, gliding to the wire in the Breeders' Cup Distaff of 1986. She was one of ten Breeders' Cup winners trained by D. Wayne Lukas, whose farflung stable organization had been setting records for several years. He led for the first time in 1983 and completed a decade as the leader in 1992, during which time Lukas took the all-time one-year record to a dizzying $17,842,358.

Lady's Secret, a daughter of Secretariat, was owned by the late Eugene Klein, one of Lukas's primary clients. Klein, former owner of the San Diego Chargers in the National Football League, burst upon the scene with a rough-hewn appreciation for the qualities of his horses and was leading owner in 1985 and 1987.

Klein and Lukas also teamed with Winning Colors, an Amazon of a filly that in 1988 followed Regret and Genuine Risk as the third of her gender to win the Kentucky Derby. (The Preakness and Belmont that year were won by the Secretariat colt Risen Star.)

Winning Colors returned to Churchill Downs on the darkening, wet afternoon of the Breeders' Cup there in 1988. She seemed to have scuttled the unbeaten career of Personal Ensign, but Ogden Phipps's four year old untracked herself in the slippery going. Trainer Shug McGaughey, who shepherded Personal Ensign through thirteen races in three campaigns several times interrupted by injury, was convinced that "not today" would be his press conference statement. Yet, Personal Ensign ran down the younger filly in time to win by a head. Perfection had been rescued, and polished to a high lustre.

AT RIGHT

A half-dozen of the top riders of the 1980s and 1990s: From left, Julie Krone, Jorge Velasquez, Pat Day, Laffit Pincay, Angel Cordero, Jose Santos. Photographs by Dell Hancock; Jorge Velasquez photograph by Katy Barrett.

Owner Phipps, who had raced his first stakes winner, White Cockade, some fifty-five years earlier, also had Easy Goer in his powerful stable at that time. He led owners in both 1988 and 1989. (The record of $5,858,168 that Phipps set in 1988 was eclipsed in 1991, when Ernie Samuel's Sam-Son Farm stable, led by Dance Smartly, earned $6,881,902.)

Most spectacular of Breeders' Cup victories was that of Arazi, Allen Paulson's little chestnut colt. Arazi's knees had frightened away buyers as a yearling, but he won consistently in France. Paulson instructed trainer Francois Boutin to return him to Kentucky for the Breeders' Cup. At Churchill Downs,

Arazi drew the outside post, fell back to last, but circled the field and came abreast of Bertrando. For a fleeting moment, a duel seemed in the offing, but Arazi had hit a gear seldom seen. He had already had an amazing trip, and yet he seemed launched anew. As Arazi traveled to the wire, jockey Pat Valenzuela was pulling him up, as if to prolong the raining cheers. Sheikh Mohammed, of the Maktoums, purchased a half-interest in Arazi, bringing to mind comparisons with Secretariat. When Boutin returned him next to Kentucky, the three year old of 1992 would not prove the super horse after all, but Arazi had lent one moment to the age.

ON FOLLOWING PAGE
The first turn of the 1993 Kentucky Derby. Courtesy Churchill Downs Inc./Kinetic Corporation.

ON PAGE 171
Paul Mellon (left) receives the Derby trophy from Kentucky Governor Brereton Jones after Sea Hero's triumph. Mellon is the first owner to have won the Epsom Derby and Prix de l 'Arc de Triomphe (with Mill Reef), the top races in England and France, as well as the Kentucky Derby. Courtesy Churchill Downs Inc./Kinetic Corporation.

CHARTS

AT LEFT

Photograph by Norman Mauskopf.

	TWO YEAR OLD		THREE YEAR OLD		HANDICAP DIVISION	
YEAR	MALE	FEMALE	MALE	FEMALE	MALE	FEMALE
1936	Pompoon	Apogee	Granville		Discovery	
1937	Menow	Jacola	War Admiral		Seabiscuit	
1938	El Chico	Inscoelda	Stagehand		Seabiscuit	Marica
1939	Bimelech	Now What	Challedon	Unerring	Kayak II	Lady Maryland
1940	Our Boots Whirlaway	Level Best	Bimelech		Challedon	War Plumage
1941	Alsab	Petrify	Whirlaway	Painted Veil	Mioland Big Pebble	Fairy Chant
1942	Count Fleet	Askmenow	Alsab	Vagrancy	Whirlaway	Vagrancy
1943	Platter Occupy	Durazna Twilight Tear	Count Fleet	Stefanita	Market Wise Devil Diver	Mar-Kell
1944	Pavot	Busher	By Jimminy	Twilight Tear	Devil Diver	Twilight Tear
1945	Star Pilot	Beaugay	Fighting Step	Busher	Stymie	Busher
1946	Double Jay Education	First Flight	Assault	Bridal Flower	Armed	Gallorette
1947	Citation	Bewitch	Phalanx	But Why Not	Armed	But Why Not
1948	Blue Peter	Myrtle Charm	Citation	Miss Request	Citation Shannon II	Conniver
1949	Hill Prince Oil Capitol	Bed o' Roses	Capot	Two Lea Wistful	Coaltown	Bewitch
1950	Battlefield	Aunt Jinny	Hill Prince	Next Move	Noor	Two Lea
1951	Tom Fool	Rose Jet	Counterpoint	Kiss Me Kate	Hill Prince Citation	Bed o' Roses
1952	Native Dancer	Sweet Patootie	One Count	Real Delight	Crafty Admiral	Real Delight Next Move
1953	Porterhouse Hasty Road	Evening Out	Native Dancer	Grecian Queen	Tom Fool	Sickle's Image
1954	Nashua	High Voltage	High Gun	Parlo	Native Dancer	Lavender Hill Parlo

CHAMPIONS BY SEASONS CLASSIFIED BY CATEGORY

YEAR	SPRINTER	GRASS HORSE		STEEPLECHASER	HORSE OF THE YEAR
		MALE	FEMALE		
1936	Myrtlewood			Bushranger	Granville
1937				Jungle King	War Admiral
1938					Seabiscuit
1939					Challedon
1940					Challedon
1941				Speculate	Whirlaway
1942				Elkridge	Whirlaway
1943				Brother Jones	Count Fleet
1944				Rouge Dragon	Twilight Tear
1945				Mercator	Busher
1946				Elkridge	Assault
1947	Polynesian			War Battle	Armed
1948	Coaltown			American Way	Citation
1949	Delegate			Trough Hill	Capot
	Royal Governor				Coaltown
1950	Sheilas Reward			Oedipus	Hill Prince
1951	Sheilas Reward			Oedipus	Counterpoint
1952	Tea-Maker			Oedipus	One Count
				Jam	Native Dancer
1953	Tom Fool	Iceberg II		The Mast	Tom Fool
1954	White Skies	Stan		King Commander	Native Dancer

YEAR	TWO YEAR OLD MALE	FEMALE	THREE YEAR OLD MALE	FEMALE	HANDICAP DIVISION MALE	FEMALE
1955	Needles	Doubledogdare	Nashua	Misty Morn	High Gun	Parlo
	Nail	Nasrina				Misty Morn
1956	Barbizon	Leallah	Needles	Doubledogdare	Swaps	Blue Sparkler
		Romanita				
1957	Jewel's Reward	Idun	Bold Ruler	Bayou	Dedicate	Pucker Up
	Nadir					
1958	First Landing	Quill	Tim Tam	Idun	Round Table	Bornastar
1959	Warfare	My Dear Girl	Sword Dancer	Silver Spoon	Round Table	Tempted
				Royal Native	Sword Dancer	
1960	Hail to Reason	Bowl of Flowers	Kelso	Berlo	Bald Eagle	Royal Native
1961	Crimson Satan	Cicada	Carry Back	Bowl of Flowers	Kelso	Airmans Guide
	Ridan					
1962	Never Bend	Smart Deb	Jaipur	Cicada	Kelso	Primonetta
		Affectionately				
1963	Hurry to Market	Tosmah	Chateaugay	Lamb Chop	Kelso	Cicada
	Raise a Native	Castle Forbes				
1964	Bold Lad	Queen Empress	Northern Dancer	Tosmah	Kelso	Tosmah
						Old Hat
1965	Buckpasser	Moccasin	Tom Rolfe	What a Treat	Roman Brother	Old Hat
						Affectionately
1966	Successor	Regal Gleam	Buckpasser	Lady Pitt	Buckpasser	Open Fire
		Mira Femme			Bold Bidder	Summer Scandal
1967	Vitriolic	Queen of the Stage	Damascus	Furl Sail	Damascus	Straight Deal
				Gamely	Buckpasser	
1968	Top Knight	Process Shot	Stage Door Johnny	Dark Mirage	Dr. Fager	Gamely
		Gallant Bloom	Forward Pass			
1969	Silent Screen	Fast Attack	Arts and Letters	Gallant Bloom	Arts and Letters	Gamely
		Tudor Queen			Nodouble	

YEAR	SPRINTER	GRASS HORSE		STEEPLECHASER	HORSE OF THE YEAR
		MALE	FEMALE		
1955	Berseem	St. Vincent		Neji	Nashua
1956	Decathlon	Career Boy		Shipboard	Swaps
1957	Decathlon	Round Table		Neji	Bold Ruler
					Dedicate
1958	Bold Ruler	Round Table		Neji	Round Table
1959	Intentionally	Round Table		Ancestor	Sword Dancer
1960				Benguala	Kelso
1961		T. V. Lark		Peal	Kelso
1962				Barnabys Bluff	Kelso
1963		Mongo		Amber Diver	Kelso
1964				Bon Nouvel	Kelso
1965	Affectionately	Parka		Bon Nouvel	Roman Brother
					Moccasin
1966	Impressive	Assagai		Tuscalee	Buckpasser
				Mako	
1967	Dr. Fager	Fort Marcy		Quick Pitch	Damascus
1968	Dr. Fager	Dr. Fager		Bon Nouvel	Dr. Fager
		Fort Marcy			
1969	Ta Wee	Hawaii		L'Escargot	Arts and Letters

YEAR	TWO YEAR OLD		THREE YEAR OLD		HANDICAP DIVISION	
	MALE	FEMALE	MALE	FEMALE	MALE	FEMALE
1970	Hoist the Flag	Forward Gal	Personality	Office Queen	Fort Marcy	Shuvee
				Fanfreluche	Nodouble	
1971	Riva Ridge	Numbered Account	Canonero II	Turkish Trousers	Ack Ack	Shuvee
1972	Secretariat	La Prevoyante	Key to the Mint	Susan's Girl	Autobiograpy	Typecast
1973	Protagonist	Talking Picture	Secretariat	Desert Vixen	Riva Ridge	Susan's Girl
1974	Foolish Pleasure	Ruffian	Little Current	Chris Evert	Forego	Desert Vixen
1975	Honest Pleasure	Dearly Precious	Wajima	Ruffian	Forego	Susan's Girl
1976	Seattle Slew	Sensational	Bold Forbes	Revidere	Forego	Proud Delta
1977	Affirmed	Lakeville Miss	Seattle Slew	Our Mims	Forego	Cascapedia
1978	Spectacular Bid	Candy Eclair	Affirmed	Tempest Queen	Seattle Slew	Late Bloomer
		It's in the Air				
1979	Rockhill Native	Smart Angle	Spectacular Bid	Davona Dale	Affirmed	Waya
1980	Lord Avie	Heavenly Cause	Temperence Hill	Genuine Risk	Spectacular Bid	Glorious Song
1981	Deputy Minister	Before Dawn	Pleasant Colony	Wayward Lass	John Henry	Relaxing
1982	Roving Boy	Landaluce	Conquistador Cielo	Christmas Past	Lemhi Gold	Track Robbery
1983	Devil's Bag	Althea	Slew o' Gold	Heartlight No. One	Bates Motel	Ambassador of Luck
1984	Chief's Crown	Outstandingly	Swale	Life's Magic	Slew o' Gold	Princess Rooney
1985	Tasso	Family Style	Spend a Buck	Mom's Command	Vanlandingham	Life's Magic
1986	Capote	Brave Raj	Snow Chief	Tiffany Lass	Turkoman	Lady's Secret
1987	Forty Niner	Epitome	Alysheba	Sacahuista	Ferdinand	North Sider
1988	Easy Goer	Open Mind	Risen Star	Winning Colors	Alysheba	Personal Ensign
1989	Rhythm	Go for Wand	Sunday Silence	Open Mind	Blushing John	Bayakoa
1990	Fly So Free	Meadow Star	Unbridled	Go for Wand	Criminal Type	Bayakoa
1991	Arazi	Pleasant Stage	Hansel	Dance Smartly	Black Tie Affair	Queena
1992	Gilded Time	Eliza	A. P. Indy	Saratoga Dew	Pleasant Tap	Paseana

| YEAR | SPRINTER | GRASS HORSE | | STEEPLECHASER | HORSE OF THE YEAR |
		MALE	FEMALE		
1970	Ta Wee	Fort Marcy		Top Bid	Fort Marcy
					Personality
1971	Ack Ack	Run the Gantlet		Shadow Brook	Ack Ack
1972	Chou Croute	Cougar II		Soothsayer	Secretariat
1973	Shecky Greene	Secretariat		Athenian Idol	Secretariat
1974	Forego		Dahlia	Gran Kan	Forego
1975	Gallant Bob	Snow Knight		Life's Illusion	Forego
1976	My Juliet	Youth		Straight and True	Forego
1977	What a Summer	Johnny D.		Cafe Prince	Seattle Slew
1978	J. O. Tobin	Mac Diarmida		Cafe Prince	Affirmed
	Dr. Patches				
1979	Star de Naskra	Bowl Game	Trillion	Martie's Anger	Affirmed
1980	Plugged Nickle	John Henry	Just a Game	Zaccio	Spectacular Bid
1981	Guilty Conscience	John Henry	De La Rose	Zaccio	John Henry
1982	Gold Beauty	Perrault	April Run	Zaccio	Conquistador Cielo
1983	Chinook Pass	John Henry	All Along	Flatterer	All Along
1984	Eillo	John Henry	Royal Heroine	Flatterer	John Henry
1985	Precisionist	Cozzene	Pebbles	Flatterer	Spend a Buck
1986	Smile	Manila	Estrapade	Flatterer	Lady's Secret
1987	Groovy	Theatrical	Miesque	Inlander	Ferdinand
1988	Gulch	Sunshine Forever	Miesque	Jimmy Lorenzo	Alysheba
1989	Safely Kept	Steinlen	Brown Bess	Highland Bud	Sunday Silence
1990	Housebuster	Itsallgreektome	Laugh and Be Merry	Morley Street	Criminal Type
1991	Housebuster	Tight Spot	Miss Alleged	Morley Street	Black Tie Affair
1992	Rubiano	Sky Classic	Flawlessly	Lonesome Glory	A. P. Indy

FIVE FURLONGS — DIRT

TIME	HORSE, AGE, WEIGHT	TRACK, YEAR
:59	George F. Smith, 4, 100	San Francisco, 1895
:58 3/5	Jack Hunnally, 3, 108	Oakland, 1907
	Silver Stocking, 4, 102	Seattle, 1908
:58	Tern's Trick, 3, 97	Oakland, 1910
:57 1/5	Pan Zareta, 5, 120	Juarez, 1915
:57	Encantadora, 3, 115	Centennial, 1951
	Miss Todd, 2, 119	Hollywood, 1955
:56 3/5	Lucky Mel, 2, 122	Hollywood, 1956
	Bettyanbull, 4, 118	Turf Paradise, 1958
:56 2/5	Bettyanbull, 5, 120	Turf Paradise, 1959
	Soldier Girl, 3, 116	Del Mar, 1964
:56 1/5	Nancycee, 4, 113	Turf Paradise, 1966
:55 2/5	Zip Pocket, 3, 122	Turf Paradise, 1967
	Big Volume, 4, 120	Fresno District Fair, 1977
:55 1/5	Chinook Pass, 3, 113	Longacres, 1982

SIX FURLONGS — DIRT

TIME	HORSE, AGE, WEIGHT	TRACK, YEAR
1:12 3/4	Diggs, 2, 83	Chicago, 1894
1:12	Bummer, 4, 80	Kinloch, 1900
	Lux Casta, 3, 111	Brighton Beach, 1902
1:11 4/5	Dick Welles, 3, 109	Washington Park, 1903
	Ivan the Terrible, 2, 92	Worth, 1904
1:11 3/5	Roseben, 4, 147	Belmont, 1905
	Col. Bob, 2, 92	Santa Anita, 1907
1:11	Chapultepec, 3, 112	Santa Anita, 1908
	Prince Ahmed, 5, 117	Empire City, 1909
	Priscillian, 6, 113	Hamilton, 1911
1:10 4/5	Iron Mask, 5, 127	Douglas Park, 1913
	Leochares, 3, 109	Douglas Park, 1913
	Orb, 2, 90	Juarez, 1913
1:09 3/5	Iron Mask, 6, 115	Juarez, 1914
1:09 1/5	Clang, 3, 110	Coney Island (O.), 1935
	Mafosta, 4, 116	Longacres, 1946
	Polynesian, 4, 126	Atlantic City, 1946
1:08 2/5	Fair Truckle, 4, 119	Golden Gate, 1947
TIME	HORSE, AGE, WEIGHT	TRACK, YEAR
1:08 1/5	Bolero, 4, 122	Golden Gate, 1950
1:08	Dumpty Humpty, 4, 115	Golden Gate, 1957
1:07 4/5	Crazy Kid, 4, 118	Del Mar, 1962
	Admirably, 3, 122	Golden Gate, 1965
1:07 2/5	Zip Pocket, 2, 120	Turf Paradise, 1966
	Vale of Tears, 6, 120	Ak-Sar-Ben, 1969
1:07 1/5	Grey Papa, 6, 116	Longacres, 1972
	Petro D. Jay, 6, 120	Turf Paradise, 1982
1:06 4/5	Zany Tactics, 6, 126	Turf Paradise, 1987

SEVEN FURLONGS — DIRT

1:25 2/5	Clifford, 4, 127	Sheepshead Bay, 1894
1:25	The Musketeer, 4, 108	Saratoga, 1902
1:22	Roseben, 5, 126	Belmont, 1906
	Clang, 3, 105	Arlington Park, 1935
	High Resolve, 4, 126	Hollywood, 1945
1:21 4/5	Honeymoon, 4, 114	Hollywood, 1947
	Buzfuz, 5, 120	Hollywood, 1947
1:21 2/5	Ky. Colonel, 3, 116	Washington Park, 1949
1:21	Bolero, 5, 121	Santa Anita, 1951
1:20 3/5	Imbros, 4, 118	Santa Anita, 1954
1:20	El Drag, 4, 115	Hollywood, 1955
	Native Diver, 6, 126	Hollywood, 1965
1:19 4/5	Triple Bend, 4, 123	Hollywood, 1972
1:19 2/5	Rich Cream, 5, 118	Hollywood, 1980
	Time To Explode, 3, 117	Hollywood, 1982

ONE MILE — DIRT

1:38 3/4	Libertine, 3, 90	Chicago, 1894
1:37 1/4	Kildeer, 4, 91	■Monmouth, 1892
◆1:35 1/2	Salvator, 4, 110	■Monmouth, 1890
1:38	Voter, 6, 122	Brighton Beach, 1900
	Orimar, 6, 109	Washington Park, 1900
1:37 4/5	Brigadier, 4, 112	Sheepshead Bay, 1901
1:37 2/5	Dick Welles, 3, 112	Harlem, 1903
	Kiamesha, 3, 104	Belmont, 1905

Time	Horse, Age, Weight	Track, Year
1:37 ⅕	Centre Shot, 3, 105	Santa Anita, 1908
	Manasseh, 4, 93	Juarez, 1913
	Vested Rights, 3, 105	Juarez, 1913
1:36 ¼	Amalfi, 6, 107	Syracuse, 1914
1:36 ⅕	Sun Briar, 3, 113	Saratoga, 1918
1:34 ⅗	Roamer, 7, 110	Saratoga, 1918
1:36 ⅕	Fairy Wand, 5, 107	Saratoga, 1919
1:35 ⅘	Man o' War, 3, 118	Belmont, 1920
1:35 ⅗	Audacious, 5, 118	Belmont, 1921
1:35 ⅖	Cherry Pie, 3, 113	Belmont, 1923
1:35	Jack High, 4, 110	Belmont, 1930
1:34 ⅖	Equipoise, 4, 128	Arlington, 1932
	Prevaricator, 5, 118	Golden Gate, 1948
1:34	Coaltown, 4, 130	Washington Park, 1949
1:33 ⅗	Citation, 5, 128	Golden Gate, 1950
1:33 ⅕	Swaps, 4, 128	Hollywood, 1956
	Intentionally, 3, 121	Washington Park, 1959
	Pia Star, 4, 112	Arlington, 1965
1:32 ⅗	Buckpasser, 3, 125	Arlington, 1966
1:32 ⅕	Dr. Fager, 4, 134	Arlington, 1968

ONE MILE AND ONE-SIXTEENTH — DIRT

Time	Horse, Age, Weight	Track, Year
1:45 ½	Yo Tambien, 3, 99	Chicago, 1892
1:45	Carnero, 5, 107	Hawthorne, 1899
1:44 ⅘	Hyphen, 3, 102	Brighton Beach, 1902
1:44 ⅗	Glassful, 3, 101	Washington Park, 1903
	Israelite, 4, 101	Brighton Beach, 1905
1:44 ⅕	Royal Tourist, 3, 104	Oakland, 1908
1:43 ⅗	Gretna Green, 5, 100	Fort Erie, 1909
	Trap Rock, 3, 112	Fort Erie, 1911
1:42 ¾	Celesta, 4, 108	Syracuse, 1914
1:42 ⅕	Dot, 3, 100	Belmont, 1923
1:42	Top Row, 3, 109	Bay Meadows, 1934
	Bull Reigh, 5, 121	Bay Meadows, 1943
1:41 ⅗	Snow Boots, 4, 117	Santa Anita, 1946
1:41	Count Speed, 4, 122	Golden Gate, 1947
	Imbros, 4, 118	Hollywood, 1954

Time	Horse, Age, Weight	Track, Year
1:40 ⅖	Swaps, 3, 115	Hollywood, 1955
1:39	Swaps, 4, 130	Hollywood, 1956
1:38 ⅖	Hoedown's Day, 5, 119	Bay Meadows, 1983

ONE MILE AND ONE-EIGHTH — DIRT

Time	Horse, Age, Weight	Track, Year
1:51 ½	Tristan, 6, 114	New York Jockey Club, 1891
1:51 ⅕	Watercure, 3, 100	Brighton Beach, 1900
	Roechampton, 3, 94	Brighton Beach, 1901
1:51	Bonnibert, 4, 120	Brighton Beach, 1902
1:50 ⅗	Charles Edward, 3, 126	Brighton Beach, 1907
1:50	Vox Populi, 4, 110	Santa Anita, 1908
1:49 ⅗	Roamer, 3, 124	Laurel, 1914
1:49 ⅖	Borrow, 9, 117	Aqueduct, 1917
	Boots, 6, 127	Aqueduct, 1917
1:49 ⅕	Man o' War, 3, 126	Aqueduct, 1920
1:49	Goaler, 5, 94 1/2	Belmont, 1921
	Grey Lag, 3, 123	Aqueduct, 1921
1:48 ⅘	Chilhowee, 3, 115	Latonia, 1924
1:48 ⅗	Peanuts, 4, 114	Aqueduct, 1926
1:48 ⅖	Hot Toddy, 4, 110	Belmont, 1929
	Blessed Event, 4, 111	Hialeah, 1934
1:48 ⅕	Discovery, 4, 123	Aqueduct, 1935
1:47 ⅗	Indian Broom, 3, 94	Tanforan, 1936
	Shannon II, 7, 124	Golden Gate, 1948
	Coaltown, 4, 114	Hialeah, 1949
1:46 ⅘	Noor, 5, 123	Golden Gate, 1950
	Alidon, 4, 116	Hollywood, 1955
	Swaps, 4, 130	Hollywood, 1956
	Gen. Duke, 3, 122	Gulfstream, 1957
	Round Table, 4, 130	Santa Anita, 1958
1:46 ⅖	Bug Brush, 4, 113	Santa Anita, 1959
	Colorado King, 5, 119	Hollywood, 1964
	Quicken Tree, 5, 120	Del Mar, 1968
	Ole Bob Bowers, 5, 114	Bay Meadows, 1968
1:46 ⅕	Figonero, 4, 124	Del Mar, 1969
1:45 ⅖	Secretariat, 3, 124,	Belmont, 1973
1:45	Simply Majestic, 4, 114	Golden Gate, 1988

EVOLUTION OF TIME RECORDS

ONE MILE AND A QUARTER — DIRT

TIME	HORSE, AGE, WEIGHT	TRACK, YEAR
2:05	Salvator, 4, 122	Sheepshead Bay, 1890
	Morello, 3, 117	Chicago, 1893
2:03 ¾	Banquet, 3, 108	■Monmouth, 1890
2:04	Charentus, 6, 106	Yonkers, 1900
2:03 ⅘	Gold Heels, 4, 126	Brighton Beach, 1902
2:03 ⅕	Waterboy, 4, 124	Brighton Beach, 1903
2:02 ⅘	Broomstick, 3, 104	Brighton Beach, 1904
	Olambala, 4, 122	Sheepshead Bay, 1910
2:00	Whisk Broom II, 6, 139	Belmont, 1913
	Cover Up, 4, 117	Hollywood, 1947
1:59 ⅘	Shannon II, 7, 124	Golden Gate, 1948
	Coaltown, 4, 128	Gulfstream, 1949
1:58 ⅕	Noor, 5, 127	Golden Gate, 1950
	Quack, 3, 115	Hollywood, 1972
1:57 ⅘	Spectacular Bid, 4, 126	Santa Anita, 1980

ONE MILE AND ONE-HALF — DIRT

TIME	HORSE, AGE, WEIGHT	TRACK, YEAR
2:32 ¾	Lamplighter, 3, 109	Monmouth, 1892
2:30 ¼	Goodrich, 3, 102	Washington, 1898
2:29 ⅗	Thunderclap, 3, 108	Laurel, 1919
2:28 ⅘	Man o' War, 3, 118	Belmont, 1920
2:28 ⅗	Handy Mandy, 3, 109	Latonia, 1927
	War Admiral, 3, 126	Belmont, 1937
2:28 ⅖	Sorteado, 4, 112	Belmont, 1939
2:27 ⅗	Bolingbroke, 5, 115	Belmont, 1942
2:26 ⅗	Gallant Man, 3, 126	Belmont, 1957
2:26 ⅕	Going Abroad, 4, 116	Aqueduct, 1964
2:24	Secretariat, 3, 126	Belmont, 1973

TWO MILES — DIRT

TIME	HORSE, AGE, WEIGHT	TRACK, YEAR
3:27 ½	Ten Broeck, 5, 110	Louisville, 1877
	Newton, 4, 107	Washington Park, 1893
3:26 ½	Judge Denny, 5, 105	Oakland, 1898
3:25 ⅘	Fitz Herbert, 3, 106	Pimlico, 1909
3:25 ⅗	Everett, 3, 107	Pimlico, 1910
3:21 ⅘	Exterminator, 5, 128	Belmont, 1920
3:20 ⅘	Market Wise, 3, 114	Belmont, 1941
3:20 ⅖	Nashua, 4, 124	Belmont, 1956
3:19 ⅖	Kelso, 3, 119	Aqueduct, 1960

FIVE FURLONGS — TURF

TIME	HORSE, AGE, WEIGHT	TRACK, YEAR
1:00	Voorhees, 2, 117	Sheepshead Bay, 1905
:59 ⅕	Helen May, 5, 109	Monmouth, 1952
:58 ⅘	Staretta, 4, 112	Laurel, 1961
:58	Happy Angle, 5, 122	Arlington, 1963
:57 ⅘	Super Charged, 2, 119	Pimlico, 1964
:57 ⅖	Canal, 5, 119	Monmouth, 1966
	Sikkum, 4, 122	Laurel, 1967
	Mr. Joe F., 2, 122	Hollywood, 1968
	Baitman, 7, 112	Monmouth, 1968
:56 ⅖	Time To Leave, 4, 119	Hollywood, 1969
	Canterbury Road, 4, 114	Hollywood, 1969
:56	Reb's Policy, 4, 114	Hollywood, 1971
	Black Tornado, 5, 119	Golden Gate, 1975
	L'Natural, 4, 114	Golden Gate, 1977
	Neat Claim, 5, 113	Golden Gate, 1977
	Silk Or Satin, 3, 113	Penn National, 1978
	Jiva Coolit, 7, 108	Penn National, 1979
:55 ⅘	Beautiful Glass, 3, 113	Hollywood, 1982
:55 ⅖	Consent, 3, 115	Meadowlands, 1989
	Twosies Answer, 3, 116	Meadowlands, 1990
:54 ⅕	Klassy Briefcase, 6, 115	Monmouth, 1991

SIX FURLONGS — TURF

TIME	HORSE, AGE, WEIGHT	TRACK, YEAR
1:12 ⅘	Etherial, 2, 89	Sheepshead Bay, 1908
1:10 ⅘	Slick Pigeon, 3, 118	Washington Park, 1949
1:10 ⅖	Better Buy, 4, 122	Washington Park, 1950
1:10	Adaption, 3, 107	Washington Park, 1952
1:09 ⅘	Burnt Child, 5, 113	Washington Park, 1956
	Hoop Band, 5, 116	Washington Park, 1958
1:09 ⅖	Benedicto, 4, 119	Washington Park, 1959
1:08 ⅘	Canal, 8, 116	Woodbine, 1969
1:08 ⅗	Out of Hock, 3, 106	Belmont, 1982

Time	Horse, Age, Weight	Track, Year
1:08	Out of Hock, 4, 117	Belmont, 1983
1:07 ⅗	Zany Tactics, 5, 117	Hollywood, 1986
1:07	Answer Do, 4, 115	Hollywood, 1990

SEVEN FURLONGS — TURF

Time	Horse, Age, Weight	Track, Year
1:27	Hugh Penny, 5, 119	Sheepshead Bay, 1895
1:25 ⅗	Bright Arc, 4, 108	Fair Grounds, 1942
1:25	Fate, 10, 117	Hawthorne, 1949
	Warsick, 4, 114	Hawthorne, 1950
1:24 ⅗	Whirling Dough, 5, 110	Hawthorne, 1951
	Officious, 4, 116	Hawthorne, 1952
	Jet Fleet, 4, 113	Hawthorne, 1952
1:24	Logo, 4, 114	Hawthorne, 1953
1:23 ⅕	Summer Solstice, 3, 110	Hawthorne, 1955
	Lofty Peak, 4, 116	Pimlico, 1956
1:21 ⅘	Royal Mustang Jr., 4, 112	Waterford Park, 1960
1:21 ⅗	Dead Ahead, 3, 114	Belmont, 1962
	Rocky Mount, 5, 121	Belmont, 1972
1:21 ⅕	Right On, 4, 116	Belmont, 1973
1:20 ⅘	Beau Bugle, 4, 112	Belmont, 1974
	Red Wing Dream, 4, 119	Belmont, 1985
1:20 ⅕	Unduplicated, 3, 116	Woodbine, 1991

ONE MILE — TURF

Time	Horse, Age, Weight	Track, Year
1:38 ⅕	Royal Ruffin, 5, 110	Hialeah, 1933
1:39	Big Beau, 5, 108	Arlington, 1934
1:36 ⅖	Diamond Dick, 5, 114	Detroit, 1946
1:36 ⅕	Porter's Broom, 4, 126	Fair Grounds, 1948
1:35 ⅗	Volcanic, 4, 125	Hawthorne, 1949
1:35 ⅕	Inseparable, 7, 109	Hawthorne, 1952
	Dogoon, 5, 117	Hawthorne, 1957
1:34 ⅘	Roman Spark, 5, 111	Laurel, 1961
1:34 ⅗	Vimy Ridge, 3, 110	Laurel, 1962
1:34	Portsmouth, 3, 116	Laurel, 1965
	Fiddle Isle, 5, 126	Hollywood, 1970
	Step Forward, 4, 114	Gulfstream Park, 1976

Time	Horse, Age, Weight	Track, Year
1:34	Clout, 4, 114	Belmont, 1976
1:33	Poison Ivory, 4, 115	Belmont, 1979
1:32 ⅗	Royal Heroine, 4, 123	Hollywood, 1984
1:32 ⅖	Expensive Decision, 4, 112	Belmont, 1990
	Known Ranger (Eng.), 5, 113	Belmont, 1991

ONE MILE AND ONE-SIXTEENTH — TURF

Time	Horse, Age, Weight	Track, Year
1:45 ⅖	Dark Woman, 4, 105	Arlington Park, 1936
1:44	Take Wing, 5, 116	Washington Park, 1943
1:43 ⅕	Grasshopper II, 7, 112	Hialeah, 1944
1:42 ⅖	Turbine, 7, 112	Detroit, 1949
1:41 ⅘	Howdy Baby, 4, 111	Arlington Park, 1956
1:41	One-Eyed King, 5, 112	Gulfstream Park, 1959
	Eurasia, 6, 122	Gulfstream Park, 1962
1:40 ⅘	Charabanc, 5, 108	Delaware, 1963
	Red Dog, 5, 108	Delaware, 1964
1:40	Assagai, 3, 115	Saratoga, 1966
1:39 ⅘	Pretense, 4, 128	Hollywood, 1967
1:39 ⅖	Big Shot II, 5, 111	Saratoga, 1970
1:39 ⅕	Fleet Victress, 5, 115	Belmont, 1977
1:38	Told, 4, 123	Penn National, 1980

ONE MILE AND ONE-EIGHTH — TURF

Time	Horse, Age, Weight	Track, Year
1:52 ⅖	Even Up, 6, 111	Arlington Park, 1935
1:51	Take Wing, 4, 114	Washington Park, 1942
	Valdina Foe, 4, 118	Washington Park, 1944
1:49 ⅘	Pellicle, 4, 110	Arlington Park, 1947
1:49 ⅖	Galloway, 4, 122	Washington Park, 1948
1:49	Happy C., 6, 119	Washington Park, 1949
1:48 ⅗	Going Away, 4, 110	Atlantic City, 1950
1:48 ⅖	Abbe Sting, 5, 110	Arlington Park, 1953
1:47 ⅖	Poona II, 3, 108	Santa Anita, 1954
1:46 ⅘	Fleet Nasrullah, 5, 122	Santa Anita, 1960
1:46 ⅗	Geechee Lou, 5, 112	Santa Anita, 1961
	Kelso, 7, 118	Saratoga, 1964
1:45 ⅘	Pink Pigeon, 4, 116	Santa Anita, 1968
1:45 ⅖	Tentam, 4, 118	Saratoga, 1973

Time	Horse, Age, Weight	Track, Year
	Waya, 4, 115	Saratoga, 1978
	Yankee Affair, 6 ,125	Woodbine, 1988
	Crystal Water, 4, 116	Santa Anita, 1977
1:44 ⅘	Frosty the Snowman, 4, 121	Woodbine, 1989
	Exclusive Partner, 8, 121	Santa Anita, 1990
1:43 ⅘	Kostroma (Ire), 5, 117	Santa Anita, 1991

ONE MILE AND ONE-QUARTER — TURF

Time	Horse, Age, Weight	Track, Year
2:05	Grapple, 6, 110	Sheepshead Bay, 1908
2:02 ⅖	Marriage, 6, 116	Arlington Park, 1942
2:02 ⅕	Thiercelin, 6, 120	Washington Park, 1950
2:00	Thirteen of Diamonds, 5, 124	Santa Anita, 1954
1:58 ⅘	Alidon, 4, 118	*Santa Anita, 1955
	Ekaba, 4, 118	*Santa Anita, 1958
	Roscoe Maney, 4, 112	*Santa Anita, 1958
1:58 ⅖	Round Table, 5, 132	*Santa Anita, 1959
	Batteur, 5, 121	*Santa Anita, 1965
1:58 ⅕	Pink Pigeon, 5, 123	*Santa Anita, 1969
1:58	Quilche, 6, 115	*Santa Anita, 1970
1:57 ⅗	King Pellinore, 4, 124	*Santa Anita, 1976
1:57 ⅖	Double Discount, 4, 116	*Santa Anita, 1977

ONE MILE AND ONE-HALF — TURF

Time	Horse, Age, Weight	Track, Year
2:32 ⅖	Bonnie Kelso, 3, 102	Sheepshead Bay, 1909
2:29 ⅕	Stud Poker, 5, 115	Hialeah, 1948
2:29	Chicle II, 5, 130	Hialeah, 1950
2:28 ⅘	Royal Vale, 5, 113	Hialeah, 1953
2:26	By Zeus, 4, 110	Santa Anita, 1954
2:25 ⅖	St. Vincent, 4, 122	*Santa Anita, 1955
2:24 ⅖	Pardao, 5, 118	*Santa Anita, 1963
2:23 ⅘	Kelso, 7, 126	Laurel, 1964
	Fleet Host, 4, 119	Santa Anita, 1967
2:23 ⅗	Czar Alexander, 4, 126	*Santa Anita, 1969
2:23	Fiddle Isle, 5, 124	Santa Anita, 1970
	John Henry, 5, 126	Santa Anita, 1980
2:22 ⅘	Hawkster, 3, 121	Santa Anita, 1989

TWO MILES — TURF

Time	Horse, Age, Weight	Track, Year
3:29 ⅖	Infinitate, 6, 112	Hialeah, 1936
3:29 ⅕	Good Visibility, 4, 108	Hialeah, 1937
3:27	Turntable, 4, 108	Washington Park, 1942
3:25 ⅖	Penaway, 5, 118	Arlington Park, 1953
3:18	Petrone, 5, 124	Hollywood, 1969

*Downhill course
◆Run against time
■Old Monmouth Park straight course

Note: *Where a record was broken more than once during the same year, only the fastest time is listed.*

EXEMPLARS OF RACING

George D. Widener	1971
Walter M. Jeffords, Sr.	1973
John W. Hanes	1982
Paul Mellon	1989
C. V. Whitney	1991

HORSES

Name	Year Elected	Year Foaled
Ack Ack	1986	1966
Affectionately	1989	1960
Affirmed	1980	1975
All Along	1990	1979
Alsab	1976	1939
Alydar	1989	1975
American Eclipse	1970	1814
Armed	1963	1941
Artful	1956	1902
Assault	1964	1943
Battleship	1969	1927
Bed o' Roses	1976	1947
Beldame	1956	1901
Ben Brush	1955	1893
Bewitch	1977	1945
Bimelech	1990	1937
Black Gold	1989	1921
Black Helen	1991	1932
Blue Larkspur	1957	1926
Bold Ruler	1973	1954
Bon Nouvel	1976	1960
Boston	1955	1833
Broomstick	1956	1901
Buckpasser	1970	1963
Busher	1964	1942
Bushranger	1967	1930
Cafe Prince	1985	1970
Carry Back	1975	1958
Challedon	1977	1936

Name	Year Elected	Year Foaled
Chris Evert	1988	1971
Cicada	1967	1959
Citation	1959	1945
Coaltown	1983	1945
Colin	1956	1905
Commando	1956	1898
Count Fleet	1961	1940
Dahlia	1981	1970
Damascus	1974	1964
Dark Mirage	1974	1965
Davona Dale	1985	1976
Desert Vixen	1979	1970
Devil Diver	1980	1939
Discovery	1969	1931
Domino	1955	1891
Dr. Fager	1971	1964
Elkridge	1966	1938
Emperor of Norfolk	1988	1885
Equipoise	1957	1928
Exterminator	1957	1915
Fairmount	1985	1921
Fair Play	1956	1905
Fashion	1980	1837
Firenze	1981	1884
Forego	1979	1970
Gallant Bloom	1977	1966
Gallant Fox	1957	1927
Gallant Man	1987	1954
Gallorette	1962	1942
Gamely	1980	1964
Genuine Risk	1986	1977
Good and Plenty	1956	1900
Grey Lag	1957	1918
Hamburg	1986	1895
Hanover	1955	1884
Henry of Navarre	1985	1891

Name	Year Elected	Year Foaled	Name	Year Elected	Year Foaled
Hill Prince	1991	1947	Roamer	1981	1911
Hindoo	1955	1878	Roseben	1956	1901
Imp	1965	1894	Round Table	1972	1954
Jay Trump	1971	1957	Ruffian	1976	1972
John Henry	1990	1975	Ruthless	1975	1864
Johnstown	1992	1936	Salvator	1955	1886
Jolly Roger	1965	1922	Sarazen	1957	1921
Kelso	1967	1957	Seabiscuit	1958	1933
Kentucky	1983	1861	Searching	1978	1952
Kingston	1955	1884	Seattle Slew	1981	1974
Lady's Secret	1992	1982	Secretariat	1974	1970
L'Escargot	1977	1963	Shuvee	1975	1966
Lexington	1955	1850	Silver Spoon	1978	1956
Longfellow	1971	1867	Sir Archy	1955	1805
Luke Blackburn	1956	1877	Sir Barton	1957	1916
Majestic Prince	1988	1966	Slew o' Gold	1992	1980
Man o' War	1957	1917	Spectacular Bid	1982	1976
Miss Woodford	1967	1880	Stymie	1975	1941
Myrtlewood	1979	1932	Susan's Girl	1976	1969
Nashua	1965	1952	Swaps	1966	1952
Native Dancer	1963	1950	Sword Dancer	1977	1956
Native Diver	1978	1959	Sysonby	1956	1902
Neji	1966	1950	Ten Broeck	1982	1872
Northern Dancer	1976	1961	Tim Tam	1985	1955
Oedipus	1978	1946	Tom Fool	1960	1949
Old Rosebud	1968	1911	Top Flight	1966	1929
Omaha	1965	1932	Tosmah	1984	1961
Pan Zareta	1972	1910	Twenty Grand	1957	1928
Parole	1984	1879	Twilight Tear	1963	1941
Peter Pan	1956	1904	Two Lea	1982	1946
Princess Doreen	1982	1921	War Admiral	1958	1934
Princess Rooney	1991	1980	Whirlaway	1959	1938
Real Delight	1987	1949	Whisk Broom II	1979	1907
Regret	1957	1912	Zaccio	1990	1976
Reigh Count	1978	1925	Zev	1983	1920

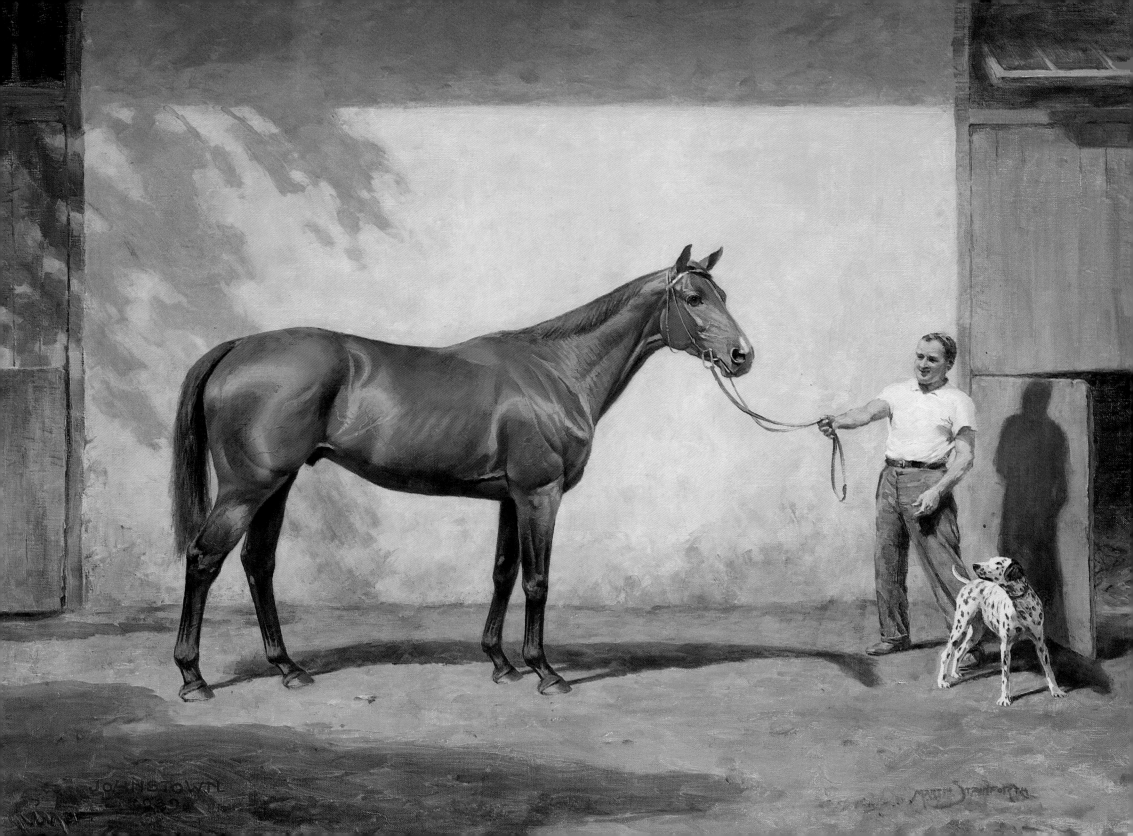

T R A I N E R S

NAME	YEAR ELECTED
Lazaro S. Barrera	1979
H. Guy Bedwell	1971
Edward D. Brown	1984
Elliott Burch	1980
Preston M. Burch	1963
W. P. Burch	1955
Fred Burlew	1973
J. D. (Dolly) Byers	1967
Frank E. Childs	1968
Henry Clark	1982
W. Burling Cocks	1985
William Duke	1956
Louis Feustel	1964
James Fitzsimmons	1958
John M. Gaver	1966
Thomas Healey	1955
Samuel Hildreth	1955
Max Hirsch	1959
W. J. (Buddy) Hirsch	1982
Thomas Hitchcock, Sr.	1973
Hollie Hughes	1973
John Hyland	1956
Hirsch Jacobs	1958
H. Allen Jerkens	1975
William R. Johnson	1986
LeRoy Jolley	1987
Ben A. Jones	1958
H. A. (Jimmy) Jones	1959
Andrew Joyner	1955
Lucien Laurin	1977
J. Howard Lewis	1969
Horatio Luro	1980

NAME	YEAR ELECTED
John E. Madden	1983
James W. Maloney	1989
Frank (Pancho) Martin	1981
Ronald McAnally	1990
Henry McDaniel	1956
MacKenzie Miller	1987
William Molter, Jr.	1960
Winbert Mulholland	1967
Edward A. Neloy	1983
John Nerud	1972
Burley Parke	1986
Angel Penna	1988
Jacob Pincus	1988
John Rogers	1955
James Rowe, Sr.	1955
Flint (Scotty) Schulhofer	1992
Jonathan Sheppard	1990
Robert A. Smith	1976
D. M. (Mike) Smithwick	1971
W. C. (Woody) Stephens	1976
Mesh Tenney	1991
H. J. Thompson	1969
Harry Trotsek	1984
Jack C. Van Berg	1985
Marion H. Van Berg	1970
Sylvester Veitch	1977
Robert W. Walden	1970
Sherrill Ward	1978
Frank Whiteley	1978
Charles Whittingham	1974
Carey Winfrey	1975
W. C. (Bill) Winfrey	1971

JOCKEYS

Name	Year Elected	Name	Year Elected
Frank (Dooley) Adams	1970●	Chris McCarron	1989
John Adams	1965	Conn McCreary	1974
Joe Aitcheson	1957●	Rigan McKinney	1968●
Edward Arcaro	1958	James McLaughlin	1955
Ted Atkinson	1957	Walter Miller	1955
Braulio Baeza	1976	Issac Murphy	1955
Carroll Bassett	1972●	Ralph Neves	1960
Walter Blum	1987	Joe Notter	1963
George H. Bostwick	1968●	George Odom	1955
Sam Boulmetis	1973	Winnie O'Connor	1956
Steve Brooks	1963	Frank O'Neill	1956
Tommy Burns	1983	Ivan Parke	1978
Jimmy Butwell	1984	Gil Patrick	1970
Frank Coltiletti	1970	Laffit Pincay, Jr.	1975
Angel Cordero, Jr.	1988	Sam Purdy	1970
Robert (Specs) Crawford	1973●	John Reiff	1956
Pat Day	1991	Alfred Robertson	1971
Lavelle (Buddy) Ensor	1962	John L. Rotz	1983
Laverne Fator	1955	Earl Sande	1955
Jerry Fishback	1992	Carroll Schilling	1970
Andrew (Mack) Garner	1969	William Shoemaker	1958
Ed (Snapper) Garrison	1955	Willie Simms	1977
Avelino Gomez	1982	Todhunter Sloan	1955
Henry Griffin	1956	A. Patrick (Paddy) Smithwick	1973●
Eric Guerin	1972	James Stout	1968
William Hartack	1959	Fred Taral	1955
Sandy Hawley	1992	Bayard Tuckerman, Jr.	1973●
Albert Johnson	1971	Ron Turcotte	1979
Willie Knapp	1969	Nash Turner	1955
Clarence Kummer	1972	Bob Ussery	1980
Charles Kurtsinger	1967	Jorge Velasquez	1990
John Loftus	1959	George Woolf	1955
John Longden	1958	Raymond Workman	1956
Danny Maher	1955	Manuel Ycaza	1977
Linus (Pony) McAtee	1956	●*Steeplechase Rider.*	

LEADING JOCKEY, TRAINER, OWNER

Year	Leading Jockeys (Races Won) (Money Won)	Leading Trainers (Races Won) (Money Won)	Leading Owners (Money Won)
1894	Simms, 228		
1895	J. Perkins, 192		
1896	J. Scherrer, 271		
1897	H. Martin, 173		
1898	T. Burns, 277		
1899	T. Burns, 273		
1900	C. Mitchell, 195		J. R. & F. P. Keene, $111,357
1901	W. O'Connor, 253		William C. Whitney, $108,440
1902	J. Ranch, 276		Green B. Morris, $98,350
1903	G. C. Fuller, 229		William C. Whitney, $102,569
1904	E. Hildebrand, 297		H. B. Duryea, $200,107
1905	D. Nicol, 221		James R. Keene, $228,724
1906	W. Miller, 388		James R. Keene, $155,519
1907	W. Miller, 334	James Rowe, 70	James R. Keene, $397,342
1908	V. Powers, 324	A. J. Joyner, 71	
	J. Notter, $464,322	James Rowe, $284,335	James R. Keene, $282,342
1909	V. Powers, 173	H. Guy Bedwell, 122	Samuel C. Hildreth, $159,112
	E. Dugan, $166,355	S. C. Hildreth, $123,942	
1910	G. Garner, 200	F. Ernest, 105	Samuel C. Hildreth, $152,645
	C. H. Shilling, $176,030	S. C. Hildreth, $148,010	
1911	T. Koerner, 162	W. B. Carson, 72	Samuel C. Hildreth, $47,473
	T. Koerner, $88,308	S. C. Hildreth, $49,418	
1912	P. Hill, 168	H. Guy Bedwell, 84	John W. Schorr, $58,225
	J. Butwell, $79,843	J. F. Schorr, $58,110	
1913	M. Buxton, 146	H. Guy Bedwell, 87	Harry Payne Whitney, $55,056
	M. Buxton, $82,552	James Rowe, $45,936	

LEADING JOCKEY, TRAINER, OWNER

YEAR	LEADING JOCKEYS (RACES WON) (MONEY WON)	LEADING TRAINERS (RACES WON) (MONEY WON)	LEADING OWNERS (MONEY WON)
1914	J. McTaggart, 157	H. Guy Bedwell, 84	John W. Schorr, $85,326
	J. McCahey, $121,845	R. C. Benson, $59,315	
1915	M. Garner, 151	H. Guy Bedwell, 97	L. S. Thompson, $104,106
	M. Garner, $96,628	James Rowe, $75,596	
1916	F. Robinson, 178	H. Guy Bedwell, 123	H. Guy Bedwell, $71,100
	J. McTaggart, $155,055	S. C. Hildreth, $70,950	
1917	W. Crump, 151	H. Guy Bedwell, 66	A. K. Macomber, $68,578
	F. Robinson, $148,057	S. C. Hildreth, $61,698	
1918	F. Robinson, 185	Kay Spence, 58	J. K. L. Ross, $99,179
	L. Luke, $201,864	H. Guy Bedwell, $80,296	
1919	C. Robinson, 190	Kay Spence, 96	J. K. L. Ross, $209,303
	J. Loftus, $252,707	H. Guy Bedwell, $208,728	
1920	J. Butwell, 152	Kay Spence, 74	Harry Payne Whitney, $270,675
	C. Kummer, $292,376	S. A. Clopton, 74	
		L. Feustel, $186,087	
1921	C. Lang, 135	S. C. Hildreth, 85	Rancocas Stable , $263,500
	E. Sande, $263,043	S. C. Hildreth, $262,768	(Harry F. Sinclair)
1922	M. Fator, 188	Henry McDaniel, 78	Rancocas Stable, $239,503
	A. Johnson, $345,054	J. A. Parsons, 78	(Harry F. Sinclair)
		S. C. Hildreth, $247,014	
1923	I. Parke, 173	C. B. Irwin, 147	Rancocas Stable, $438,849
	E. Sande, $569,394	S. C. Hildreth, $392,124	(Harry F. Sinclair)
1924	I. Parke, 205	J. A. Parson, 93	Harry Payne Whitney, $240,193
	I. Parke, $290,395	S. C. Hildreth, $255,688	
1925	A. Mortensen, 187	J. J. Duggan, 70	Glen Riddle Farm, $199,143
	L. Fator, $305,775	G. R. Tompkins, $199,245	(S. D. Riddle)

LEADING JOCKEY, TRAINER, OWNER

Year	Leading Jockeys (Races Won) (Money Won)	Leading Trainers (Races Won) (Money Won)	Leading Owners (Money Won)
1926	R. Jones, 190	W. Perkins, 82	Harry Payne Whitney, $407,139
	L. Fator, $361,435	S. P. Harlan, $205,681	
1927	L. Hardy, 207	S. C. Hildreth, 72	Harry Payne Whitney, $328,769
	E. Sande, $277,877	W. H. Bringloe, $216,563	
1928	J. Inzelone, 155	J. F. Schorr, 65	Edward B. McLean, $234,640
	L. McAtee, $301,295	J. Reed, 65	
		J. F. Schorr, $258,425	
1929	M. Knight, 149	L. Gentry, 74	Harry Payne Whitney, $362,305
	M. Garner, $314,975	J. Rowe, Jr., $314,881	
1930	H. R. Riley, 177	C. B. Irwin, 92	C. V. Whitney, $385,972
	R. Workman, $420,438	J. Fitzsimmons, $397,355	
1931	H. Roble, 173	J. C. Mikel, 72	C. V. Whitney, $422,923
	C. Kurtsinger, $392,095	J. W. Healy, $297,300	
1932	J. Gilbert, 212	G. Alexandra, 76	C. V. Whitney, $403,681
	R. Workman, $385,070	J. Fitzsimmons, $266,650	
1933	J. Westrope, 301	Hirsch Jacobs, 116	C. V. Whitney, $241,292
	R. Jones, $226,285	R. A. Smith, $135,720	
1934	M. Peters, 221	Hirsch Jacobs, 127	Brookmeade Stable, $251,138
	W. D. Wright, $287,185	R. A. Smith, $249,938	(Mrs. Dodge Sloan)
1935	C. Stevenson, 206	Hirsch Jacobs, 114	A. G. Vanderbilt, $303,605
	S. Coucci, $319,760	J. H. Stotler, $303,005	
1936	B. James, 245	Hirsch Jacobs, 177	Milky Way Farm Stable, $206,450
	W. D. Wright, $264,000	J. Fitzsimmons, $193,415	(Mrs. Ethel V. Mars)
1937	J. Adams, 260	Hirsch Jacobs, 134	Mrs. Chas. S. Howard, $214,559
	C. Kurtsinger, $384,202	R. McGarvey, $209,925	
1938	J. Longden, 236	Hirsch Jacobs, 109	H. Maxwell Howard, $226,495
	N. Wall, $385,161	E. H. Sande, $226,495	

LEADING JOCKEY, TRAINER, OWNER

YEAR	LEADING JOCKEYS (RACES WON) (MONEY WON)	LEADING TRAINERS (RACES WON) (MONEY WON)	LEADING OWNERS (MONEY WON)
1939	D. Meade, 255	Hirsch Jacobs, 106	Belair Stud, $284,250
	B. James, $353,333	J. Fitzsimmons, $266,205	(William Woodward)
1940	E. Dew, 287	D. Womeldorff, 108	Charles S. Howard, $334,120
	E. Arcaro, $343,661	T. Smith, $269,200	
1941	D. Meade, 210	Hirsch Jacobs, 123	Calumet Farm, $475,091
	D. Meade, $398,627	B. A. Jones, $475,316	(Warren Wright)
1942	J. Adams, 245	Hirsch Jacobs, 133	Greentree Stable, $414,432
	E. Arcaro, $481,949	J. M. Gaver, $406,547	(Mrs. Payne Whitney)
1943	J. Adams, 228	Hirsch Jacobs, 128	Calumet Farm, $267,915
	J. Longden, $573,276	B. A. Jones, $267,915	(Warren Wright)
1944	T. Atkinson, 287	Hirsch Jacobs, 117	Calumet Farm, $601,660
	T. Atkinson, $899,101	B. A. Jones, $601,660	(Warren Wright)
1945	J. D. Jessop, 290	S. Lipiec, 127	Maine Chance Farm, $589,170
	J. Longden, $981,977	T. Smith, $510,655	(Mrs. Elizabeth N. Graham)
1946	T. Atkinson, 233	W. Molter, 122	Calumet Farm, $564,095
	T. Atkinson, $1,036,825	Hirsch Jacobs, $560,077	(Warren Wright)
1947	J. Longden, 316	W. Molter, 155	Calumet Farm, $1,402,436
	D. Dodson, $1,429,949	H. A. Jones, $1,334,805	(Warren Wright)
1948	J. Longden, 319	W. Molter, 184	Calumet Farm, $1,269,710
	E. Arcaro, $1,686,230	H. A. Jones, $1,118,670	(Warren Wright)
1949	G. Glisson, 270	W. H. Bishop/W. Molter, 129	Calumet Farm, $1,128,942
	S. Brooks, $1,316,817	H. A. Jones, $978,587	(Warren Wright)
1950	J. Culmone/W. Shoemaker, 388	R. H. McDaniel, 156	Brookmeade Stable, $651,399
	E. Arcaro, $1,410,160	P. M. Burch, $637,754	(Mrs. Dodge Sloan)
1951	C. Burr, 310	R. H. McDaniel, 164	Greentree Stable, $637,242
	W. Shoemaker, $1,329,890	J. M. Gaver, $616,392	(Mrs. C. S. Payson & J. H. Whitney)
1952	A. DeSpirito, 390	R. H. McDaniel, 168	Calumet Farm, $1,283,197
	E. Arcaro, $1,859,591	B. A. Jones, $662,137	(Mrs. Gene Markey)

Year	Leading Jockeys (Races Won) (Money Won)	Leading Trainers (Races Won) (Money Won)	Leading Owners (Money Won)
1953	W. Shoemaker, 485	R. H. McDaniel, 211	A. G. Vanderbilt, $987,306
	W. Shoemaker, $1,784,187	H. Trotsek, $1,028,873	
1954	W. Shoemaker, 380	R. H. McDaniel, 206	King Ranch, $837,615
	W. Shoemaker, $1,876,760	W. Molter, $1,107,860	(Robert J. Kleberg, Jr.)
1955	W. Hartack, 417	F. H. Merrill, Jr., 154	Hasty House Farm, $832,879
	E. Arcaro, $1,864,796	J. Fitzsimmons, $1,270,055	(Mr. and Mrs. A. E. Reuben)
1956	W. Hartack, 347	V. R. Wright, 177	Calumet Farm, $1,057,383
	W. Hartack, $2,343,955	W. Molter, $1,227,402	(Mrs. Gene Markey)
1957	W. Hartack, 341	V. R. Wright, 192	Calumet Farm, $1,150,910
	W. Hartack, $3,060,501	H. A. Jones, $1,150,910	(Mrs. Gene Markey)
1958	W. Shoemaker, 300	F. H. Merrill, Jr., 171	Calumet Farm, $946,262
	W. Shoemaker, $2,961,693	W. Molter, $1,116,544	(Mrs. Gene Markey)
1959	W. Shoemaker, 347	V. R. Wright, 172	Cain Hoy Stable, $742,081
	W. Shoemaker, $2,843,133	W. Molter, $847,290	(H. F. Guggenheim)
1960	W. Hartack, 307	F. H. Merrill, Jr., 143	C. V. Whitney, $1,039,091
	W. Shoemaker, $2,123,961	Hirsch Jacobs, $748,349	
1961	J. Sellers, 328	V. R. Wright, 178	Calumet Farm, $759,856
	W. Shoemaker, $2,690,819	H. A. Jones, $759,856	(Mrs. Gene Markey)
1962	R. Ferraro, 352	W. H. Bishop, 162	Rex C. Ellsworth, $1,154,454
	W. Shoemaker, $2,916,844	M. A. Tenney, $1,099,474	
1963	W. Blum, 360	H. Jacobson, 140	Rex C. Ellsworth, $1,096,863
	W. Shoemaker, $2,526,925	M. A. Tenney, $860,703	
1964	W. Blum, 324	H. Jacobson, 169	Wheatley Stable, $1,073,572
	W. Shoemaker, $2,649,553	W. C. Winfrey, $1,350,534	(Mrs. Henry C. Phipps)
1965	J. Davidson, 319	H. Jacobson, 200	Marion H. Van Berg, $895,246
	B. Baeza, $2,582,702	H. Jacobs, $1,331,628	

YEAR	LEADING JOCKEYS (RACES WON) (MONEY WON)	LEADING TRAINERS (RACES WON) (MONEY WON)	LEADING OWNERS (MONEY WON)
1966	A. Gomez, 318	L. Cavalaris, Jr., 175	Wheatley Stable, $1,225,861
	B. Baeza, $2,951,022	E. A. Neloy, $2,456,250	(Mrs. Henry C. Phipps)
1967	J. Velasquez, 438	E. Hammond, 200	Hobeau Farm, $1,120,143
	B. Baeza, $3,088,888	E. A. Neloy, $1,776,089	(J. J. Dreyfus, Jr.)
1968	A. Cordero, Jr., 345	J. Van Berg, 256	Marion H. Van Berg, $1,105,388
	B. Baeza, $2,835,108	E. A. Neloy, $1,233,101	
1969	L. Snyder, 352	J. Van Berg, 239	Marion H. Van Berg, $1,453,679
	J. Velasquez, $2,542,315	Elliott Burch, $1,067,936	
1970	S. Hawley, 452	J. Van Berg, 282	Marion H. Van Berg, $1,347,289
	L. Pincay, Jr., $2,626,526	C. Whittingham, $1,302,354	
1971	L. Pincay, Jr., 380	D. Baird, 245	S. Sommer, $1,523,508
	L. Pincay, Jr., $3,784,377	C. Whittingham, $1,737,115	
1972	S. Hawley, 367	J. Van Berg, 286	S. Sommer, $1,605,896
	L. Pincay, Jr., $3,225,827	C. Whittingham, $1,734,020	
1973	S. Hawley, 515	D. Baird, 305	Dan R. Lasater, $1,498,785
	L. Pincay, Jr., $4,093,492	C. Whittingham, $1,865,385	
1974	C. McCarron, 546	J. Van Berg, 329	Dan R. Lasater, $3,022,960
	L. Pincay, Jr., $4,251,060	F. Martin, $2,408,419	
1975	C. McCarron, 468	R. E. Dutrow, 352	Dan R. Lasater, $2,894,726
	B. Baeza, $3,674,398	C. Whittingham, $2,437,244	
1976	S. Hawley, 413	J. Van Berg, 496	Dan R. Lasater, $2,894,074
	A. Cordero, Jr., $4,709,500	J. Van Berg, $2,976,196	
1977	S. Cauthen, 487	K. Leatherbury, 322	Elmendorf, $2,309,200
	S. Cauthen, $6,151,750	L. Barrera, $2,715,848	(Max Gluck)
1978	E. Delahoussaye, 384	K. Leatherbury, 304	Harbor View Farm, $2,097,443
	D. McHargue, $6,188,353	L. Barrera, $3,307,164	
1979	D. Gall, 479	D. Baird, 316	Harbor View Farm, $2,701,741
	L. Pincay, Jr., $8,183,535	L. Barrera, $3,608,517	

LEADING JOCKEY, TRAINER, OWNER

Year	Leading Jockeys (Races Won) (Money Won)	Leading Trainers (Races Won) (Money Won)	Leading Owners (Money Won)
1980	C. McCarron, 405	D. Baird, 306	Harbor View Farm, $2,207,576
	C. McCarron, $7,666,100	L. Barrera, $2,969,151	
1981	D. Gall, 376	D. Baird, 349	Elmendorf, $1,928,102
	C. McCarron, $8,397,604	C. Whittingham, $3,993,302	(Max Gluck)
1982	P. Day, 399	D. Baird, 276	Viola Sommer, $2,182,626
	A. Cordero, Jr., $9,702,520	C. Whittingham, $4,587,457	
1983	P. Day, 454	J. Van Berg, 258	John Franks, $2,643,251
	A. Cordero, Jr., $10,116,807	D. Wayne Lukas, $4,267,261	
1984	P. Day, 399	J. Van Berg, 250	John Franks, $3,070,225
	C. McCarron, $12,038,213	D. Wayne Lukas, $5,835,921	
1985	C. Antley, 469	D. Baird, 249	Mr. & Mrs. E. V. Klein, $5,451,201
	L. Pincay, Jr., $13,415,049	D. Wayne Lukas, $11,155,188	
1986	P. Day, 429	J. Van Berg, 266	John Franks, $4,463,375
	J. Santos, $11,329,297	D. Wayne Lukas, $12,345,180	
1987	K. Desormeaux, 450	D. Wayne Lukas, 343	Mr. & Mrs. E. V. Klein, $5,746,334
	J. Santos, $12,407,355	D. Wayne Lukas, $17,502,110	
1988	K. Desormeaux, 474	D. Wayne Lukas, 318	Ogden Phipps, $5,858,168
	J. Santos, $14,877,298	D. Wayne Lukas, $17,842,358	
1989	K. Desormeaux, 598	D. Wayne Lukas, 305	Ogden Phipps, $5,438,034
	J. Santos, $13,847,003	D. Wayne Lukas, $16,103,998	
1990	P. Day, 364	D. Wayne Lukas, 267	Kinghaven Farms, $5,041,280
	G. Stevens, $13,881,198	D. Wayne Lukas, $14,508,871	
1991	P. Day, 430	D. Wayne Lukas, 296	Sam-Son Farm, $6,881,902
	C. McCarron, $14,456,073	D. Wayne Lukas, $15,942,223	
1992	R. Baze, 433	D. Baird, 256	Golden Eagle Farm, $5,479,484
	K. Desormeaux, $14,193,006	D. Wayne Lukas, $9,806,436	

Year	Leading Breeders (Races Won) (Money Won)	Leading Sires (Progeny Earnings)	Year	Leading Breeders (Races Won) (Money Won)	Leading Sires (Progeny Earnings)
1894		Sir Modred, $134,318	1915		Broomstick, $94,387
1895		Hanover, $106,908	1916		Star Shoot, $138,163
1896		Hanover, $86,853	1917		Star Shoot, $131,674
1897		Hanover, $122,374	1918	John E. Madden, 213	Sweep, $139,057
1898		Hanover, $118,590	1919	John E. Madden, 311	Star Shoot, $197,233
1899		Albert, $95,975	1920	John E. Madden, 313	Fair Play, $269,102
1900		Kingston, $116,368	1921	John E. Madden, 424	Celt, $206,167
1901		Sir Dixon, $165,682	1922	John E. Madden, 366	McGee, $222,491
1902		Hastings, $113,865		John E. Madden, $568,785	
1903		Ben Strome, $106,965	1923	John E. Madden, 419	The Finn, $285,759
1904		Meddler, $222,555		John E. Madden, $623,630	
1905		Hamburg, $153,160	1924	John E. Madden, 318	Fair Play, $296,204
1906		Meddler, $151,243		Harry Payne Whitney, $482,865	
1907		Commando, $270,345	1925	John E. Madden, 383	Sweep, $237,564
1908		Hastings, $154,061		John E. Madden, $535,790	
1909		Ben Brush, $75,143	1926	John E. Madden, 368	Man o' War, $408,137
1910		Kingston, $85,220		Harry Payne Whitney, $715,158	
1911		Star Shoot, $53,895	1927	John E. Madden, 362	Fair Play, $361,518
1912		Star Shoot, $79,973		Harry Payne Whitney, $718,144	
1913		Broomstick, $76,009	1928	Himyar Stud, 331	High Time, $307,631
1914		Broomstick, $99,043		Harry Payne Whitney, $514,832	

Year	Leading Breeders (Races Won) (Money Won)	Leading Sires (Progeny Earnings)	Year	Leading Breeders (Races Won) (Money Won)	Leading Sires (Progeny Earnings)
1929	Himyar Stud, 335 Harry Payne Whitney, $825,374	Chicle, $289,123	1938	Arthur B. Hancock, 300 H. P. & C. V. Whitney, $374,049	Sickle, $327,822
1930	Audley Farm, 318 Harry Payne Whitney, $698,280	Sir Gallahad III, $422,200	1939	Willis Sharpe Kilmer, 269 Arthur B. Hancock, $345,503	Challenger II, $316,281
1931	Audley Farm, 359 Harry Payne Whitney, $582,970	St. Germans, $315,585	1940	Arthur B. Hancock, 302 J. E. Widener, $317,961	Sir Gallahad III, $305,610
1932	Himyar Stud, 267 Harry Payne Whitney Estate, $560,803	Chatterton, $210,040	1941	Willis Sharpe Kilmer, 256 Warren Wright (Calumet Farm), $528,211	Blenheim II, $378,981
1933	Harry Payne & C. V. Whitney, 282 Harry Payne & C. V. Whitney, $342,866	Sir Gallahad III, $136,428	1942	Arthur B. Hancock, 333 Mrs. Payne Whitney (Greentree Stable), $536,173	Equipoise, $437,141
1934	Harry Payne & C. V. Whitney, 310 Harry Payne & C. V. Whitney, $320,955	Sir Gallahad III, $180,165	1943	Arthur B. Hancock, 346 Arthur B. Hancock, $619,049	Bull Dog, $372,706
1935	Arthur B. Hancock, 292 Arthur B. Hancock, $359,218	Chance Play, $191,465	1944	Arthur B. Hancock, 322 Warren Wright (Calumet Farm), $990,612	Chance Play, $431,100
1936	Arthur B. Hancock, 314 Arthur B. Hancock, $362,762	Sickle, $209,800	1945	Mereworth Farm, 307 E. E. Dale Shaffer (Coldstream Stud), $791,477	War Admiral, $591,352
1937	Arthur B. Hancock, 279 Arthur B. Hancock, $416,558	The Porter, $292,262	1946	Arthur B. Hancock, 350 Mereworth Farm, $962,677	Mahmoud, $638,025

Year	Leading Breeders (Races Won) (Money Won)	Leading Sires (Progeny Earnings)	Year	Leading Breeders (Races Won) (Money Won)	Leading Sires (Progeny Earnings)
1947	Mereworth Farm, 358 Warren Wright (Calumet Farm), $1,807,432	Bull Lea, $1,259,718	1954	Calumet Farm, 201 Mrs. Gene Markey (Calumet Farm), $1,139,609	Heliopolis, $1,406,638
1948	Mereworth Farm, 330 Warren Wright (Calumet Farm), $1,559,850	Bull Lea, $1,334,027	1955	Henry H. Knight, 223 Mrs. Gene Markey (Calumet Farm), $999,737	Nasrullah, $1,433,660
1949	Mereworth Farm, 347 Warren Wright (Calumet Farm), $1,515,181	Bull Lea, $991,842	1956	Henry H. Knight, 293 Mrs. Gene Markey (Calumet Farm), $1,528,727	Nasrullah, $1,462,413
1950	Mereworth Farm, 313 Warren Wright (Calumet Farm), $1,090,286	Heliopolis, $852,292	1957	Henry H. Knight, 284 Mrs. Gene Markey (Calumet Farm), $1,469,473	Princequillo, $1,698,427
1951	Mereworth Farm, 299 Mrs. Gene Markey (Calumet Farm), $1,198,107	Count Fleet, $1,160,847	1958	Henry H. Knight, 260 Claiborne Farm, $1,414,355 (A. B. Hancock, Jr. & Sr.)	Princequillo, $1,394,540
1952	Mereworth Farm, 270 Mrs. Gene Markey (Calumet Farm), $2,060,590	Bull Lea, $1,630,655	1959	King Ranch, 227 Claiborne Farm, $1,322,595 (A. B. Hancock, Jr.)	Nasrullah, $1,434,543
1953	Mereworth Farm, 246 Mrs. Gene Markey (Calumet Farm), $1,573,803	Bull Lea, $1,155,846	1960	E. P. Taylor, 267 C. V. Whitney, $1,193,181	Nasrullah, $1,419,683

Year	Leading Breeders (Races Won) (Money Won)	Leading Sires (Progeny Earnings)	Year	Leading Breeders (Races Won) (Money Won)	Leading Sires (Progeny Earnings)
1961	E. P. Taylor, 265 Mrs. Gene Markey (Calumet Farm), $1,078,894	Ambiorix, $936,976	1969	E. P. Taylor, 302 Claiborne Farm (A. B. Hancock, Jr.), $1,331,485	Bold Ruler, $1,357,144
1962	E. P. Taylor, 263 R. C. Ellsworth, $1,678,769	Nasrullah, $1,474,831	1970	Harbor View Farm, 366 Harbor View Farm, $1,515,861	Hail to Reason, $1,400,839
1963	E. P. Taylor, 300 R. C. Ellsworth, $1,465,069	Bold Ruler, $917,531	1971	Harbor View Farm, 394 Harbor View Farm, $1,739,214	Northern Dancer, $1,288,580
1964	E. P. Taylor, 305 Bieber-Jacobs Stable (I. Bieber & H. Jacobs), $1,301,677	Bold Ruler, $1,457,156	1972	Harbor View Farm, 326 Leslie Combs II, $1,578,851	Round Table, $1,199,933
1965	E. P. Taylor, 290 Bieber-Jacobs Stable (I. Bieber & H. Jacobs), $1,994,649	Bold Ruler, $1,091,924	1973	R. C Ellsworth, 365 Elmendorf Farm (Max Gluck), $2,128,080	Bold Ruler, $1,488,622
1966	E. P. Taylor, 310 Bieber-Jacobs Stable (I. Bieber & H. Jacobs), $1,575,027	Bold Ruler, $2,306,52∃	1974	R. C. Ellsworth, 415 E. P. Taylor, $1,926,937	T. V. Lark, $1,242,000
1967	E. P. Taylor, 288 Bieber-Jacobs Stable (I. Bieber & H. Jacobs), $1,515,414	Bold Ruler, $2,249,272	1975	R. C. Ellsworth, 402 E. P. Taylor, $2,369,145	What a Pleasure, $2,011,878
1968	E. P. Taylor, 280 Claiborne Farm (A. B. Hancock, Jr.), $1,493,189	Bold Ruler, $1,988,427	1976	R. C. Ellsworth, 361 E. P. Taylor, $3,022,181	What a Pleasure, $1,622,159
			1977	E. P. Taylor, 409 E. P. Taylor, $3,414,169	Dr. Fager, $1,593,079
			1978	E. P. Taylor, 442 E. P. Taylor, $3,387,945	Exclusive Native, $1,969,867

Year	Leading Breeders (races won) (money won)	Leading Sires (progeny earnings)	Year	Leading Breeders (races won) (money won)	Leading Sires (progeny earnings)
1979	E. P. Taylor, 353 E. P. Taylor, $3,001,108	Exclusive Native, $2,872,605	1986	N. B. Hunt (Bluegrass Farm), 281 N. B. Hunt (Bluegrass Farm), $5,013,667	Lyphard, $4,051,985
1980	E. P. Taylor, 305 E. P. Taylor, $3,111,006	Raja Baba, $2,483,352	1987	N. B. Hunt (Bluegrass Farm), 324 N. B. Hunt (Bluegrass Farm), $5,095,050	Mr. Prospector, $5,877,385
1981	E. P. Taylor, 242 Elmendorf Farm (Max Gluck), $2,736,029	Nodouble, $2,800,884	1988	John Franks, 414 Ogden Phipps, $6,031,205	Mr. Prospector, $8,986,790
1982	E. P. Taylor, 233 Elmendorf Farm (Max Gluck), $3,049,444	His Majesty, $2,675,823	1989	John Franks, 486 Ogden Phipps, $5,568,537	Halo, $7,520,142
1983	E. P. Taylor, 227 E. P. Taylor, $3,472,128	Halo, $2,773,637	1990	John Franks, 451 Tartan Farms, $6,930,043	Alydar, $6,378,760
1984	E. P. Taylor, 261 Claiborne Farm, $5,554,012	Seattle Slew, $5,361,259	1991	John Franks, 491 Sam-Son Farms, $6,922,993	Danzig, $6,214,669
1985	E. P. Taylor, 241 E. P. Taylor, $4,492,453	Buckaroo, $4,145,272	1992	John Franks, 584 Mr. & Mrs. John C. Mabee, $7,026,627	Danzig, $5,873,773

R A C I N G S T A T I S T I C S

Year	Reg. Foals	Days of Racing	No. Races	No. Horses Racing	Average Purse Distribution	Average Purse Per Race	Dist. Per Horse
1895	——	——	7,362	5,456	$ 2,826,749	$ 383.96	$ 518.10
1900	3,476	——	7,226	——	——	——	——
1901	3,784	——	8,391	5,127	——	——	——
1902	3,600	——	7,483	5,271	4,662,424	623.07	884.54
1903	3,440	——	——	5,525	5,190,450	——	939.45
1904	3,990	——	8,594	5,962	5,774,689	671.94	968.58
1905	3,800	1,302	8,473	6,232	5,601,557	661.11	898.84
1906	3,840	1,236	7,657	5,962	5,420,381	708.54	909.15
1907	3,780	1,004	6,252	5,662	5,375,554	859.81	949.40
1908	3,080	921	5,699	5,405	4,351,691	763.58	805.12
1909	2,340	724	4,510	4,890	3,146,695	697.71	643.49
1910	1,950	1,063	6,501	4,180	2,942,333	452.59	703.90
1911	2,040	1,037	6,289	4,038	2,337,957	371.75	578.98
1912	1,900	926	5,806	3,553	2,391,625	411.92	673.12
1913	1,722	969	6,136	3,541	2,920,963	476.03	824.89
1914	1,702	906	5,849	3,632	2,994,525	511.97	824.48
1915	2,120	839	5,454	3,700	2,853,037	523.10	771.09
1916	2,128	1,035	6,098	3,754	3,842,471	630.11	1,023.56
1917	1,680	902	5,899	4,200	4,066,253	689.31	968.15
1918	1,950	610	3,968	3,575	3,425,347	863.24	958.13
1919	1,665	686	4,408	3,531	4,642,865	1,053.28	1,314.88
1920	1,833	1,022	6,897	4,032	7,773,407	1,127.07	1,927.92
1921	2,035	1,074	7,250	4,623	8,435,083	1,163.45	1,824.59
1922	2,352	1,182	8,045	5,049	9,096,215	1,130.66	1,801.58

Year	Reg. Foals	Days of Racing	No. Races	No. Horses Racing	Average Purse Distribution	Average Purse per Race	Dist. per Horse
1923	2,763	1,319	8,991	5,437	9,675,811	$1,076.16	$1,779.62
1924	2,921	1,456	10,007	5,906	10,825,446	1,081.78	1,741.52
1925	3,272	1,656	11,579	6,438	12,577,270	1,086.21	1,953.59
1926	3,632	1,713	12,065	7,218	13,884,820	1,150.83	1,923.63
1927	4,182	1,680	11,832	7,794	13,935,610	1,177.78	1,787.99
1928	4,503	1,613	11,465	8,171	13,332,361	1,162.87	1,631.66
1929	4,903	1,599	11,133	8,332	13,417,817	1,205.22	1,610.39
1930	5,137	1,653	11,477	8,791	13,674,160	1,191.44	1,555.47
1931	5,266	1,660	11,690	9,128	13,084,154	1,119.26	1,533.40
1932	5,256	1,518	10,835	9,017	10,082,757	930.57	1,118.19
1933	5,158	1,746	12,680	9,176	8,516,325	671.63	928.10
1934	4,924	1,959	14,261	9,470	10,443,495	732.31	1,102.79
1935	5,038	2,133	15,830	10,544	12,794,418	808.23	1,213.43
1936	5,042	2,033	15,344	10,757	12,994,605	846.88	1,208.01
1937	5,535	2,140	16,250	11,515	14,363,562	883.91	1,247.37
1938	5,696	2,140	16,243	12,185	14,946,609	920.18	1,226.64
1939	6,316	2,199	16,967	12,804	15,312,839	902.50	1,195.95
1940	6,003	2,096	16,401	13,257	15,911,167	970.13	1,200.20
1941	6,805	2,162	16,912	13,683	17,987,225	1,063.57	1,314.56
1942	6,427	2,228	17,593	12,614	18,136,118	1,030.87	1,437.77
1943	5,923	2,052	16,094	11,258	18,555,680	1,152.95	1,648.22
1944	5,650	2,396	19,228	12,959	29,159,099	1,516.49	2,250.10
1945	5,819	2,480	19,587	14,307	32,300,060	1,649.05	2,257.64
1946	6,579	3,020	23,940	17,601	49,291,024	2,058.94	2,800.46
1947	7,705	3,134	24,884	19,063	53,932,141	2,167.34	2,829.15

Year	Reg. Foals	Days of Racing	No. Races	No. Horses Racing	Average Purse Distribution	Average Purse per Race	Dist. per Horse
1948	8,434	3,183	25,388	20,254	54,436,063	$2,144.16	$2,687.66
1949	8,770	3,309	26,832	21,616	52,317,078	1,949.80	2,420.29
1950	9,095	3,290	26,932	22,554	50,102,099	1,860.31	2,221.42
1951	8,944	3,394	27,856	22,819	55,551,124	1,994.22	2,434.42
1952	8,811	3,515	29,051	23,813	63,950,236	2,201.30	2,685.51
1953	9,040	3,635	30,069	24,417	72,870,819	2,423.45	2,984.42
1954	9,064	3,685	30,467	25,294	74,255,611	2,437.24	2,935.70
1955	9,610	3,827	31,757	26,056	76,643,696	2,413.44	2,941.49
1956	10,112	3,979	33,445	26,507	81,311,581	2,431.20	3,067.55
1957	10,832	4,120	34,982	27,355	85,300,966	2,438.42	3,118.29
1958	11,377	3,910	33,325	28,099	85,467,082	2,564.65	3,041.64
1959	12,240	4,218	36,579	28,623	92,848,541	2,538.30	3,243.84
1960	12,901	4,304	37,661	29,773	93,741,552	2,489.08	3,148.54
1961	13,794	4,641	40,744	30,381	98,846,843	2,426.04	3,253.57
1962	14,870	4,772	41,766	33,579	103,525,712	2,478.71	3,083.05
1963	15,917	5,203	45,449	35,828	113,122,209	2,488.99	3,157.37
1964	17,343	5,326	46,922	37,812	121,777,847	2,595.33	3,220.61
1965	18,846	5,283	47,335	38,502	126,463,984	2,671.68	3,284.61
1966	20,228	5,254	46,814	39,604	130,653,813	2,790.91	3,299.01
1967	21,876	5,344	47,811	41,853	139,170,738	2,910.85	3,325.23
1968	22,911	5,553	49,777	43,710	150,744,478	3,026.39	3,446.45
1969	23,847	5,825	52,315	45,808	168,713,911	3,224.96	3,683.07
1970	24,361	6,242	56,676	49,087	185,625,110	3,275.20	3,781.55
1971	24,301	6,394	57,467	50,470	201,435,894	3,505.24	3,991.20
1972	25,726	6,624	59,410	52,488	210,607,082	3,544.98	4,012.48

Year	Reg. Foals	Days of Racing	No. Races	No. Horses Racing	Average Purse Distribution	Average Purse per Race	Dist. per Horse
1973	26,810	6,888	62,272	54,813	233,936,153	$3,756.68	$4,267.90
1974	27,586	7,201	65,312	56,520	263,951,376	4,500.73	4,670.05
1975	28,271	7,488	68,210	58,816	292,583,798	4,289.46	4,974.56
1976	28,809	7,593	69,480	61,084	318,963,255	4,590.72	5,221.72
1977	30,036	7,525	68,822	61,970	336,022,495	4,882.49	5,422.34
1978	31,510	7,579	69,499	62,950	367,637,193	5,289.82	5,840.15
1979	32,904	7,515	69,407	63,769	415,414,224	5,985.19	6,514.36
1980	35,679	7,443	68,252	64,519	458,225,095	6,713.72	7,102.17
1981	38,670	7,661	71,066	65,844	517,287,652	7,280.38	7,856.26
1982	42,894	7,729	71,798	69,510	537,274,475	7,483.14	7,729.46
1983	47,236	7,617	70,917	74,609	555,761,003	7,836.78	7,448.98
1984	49,244	7,995	74,021	78,267	616,829,594	8,333.17	7,881.09
1985	50,429	8,143	75,424	82,594	660,799,909	8,761.14	8,000.58
1986	51,293	8,273	77,855	86,119	682,220,684	8,762.71	7,921.84
1987	50,917	8,539	80,525	89,511	722,494,743	8,972.30	8,071.57
1988	49,216	8,488	79,710	90,517	753,205,416	9,449.32	8,321.15
1989	48,196	8,858	83,110	91,441	787,973,110	9,481.09	8,617.28
1990	44,093	8,641	81,376	91,075	796,468,772	9,787.51	8,745.20
1991	42,000 ★	8,605	80,053	86,934	783,087,383	9,782.11	9,007.84
1992	38,500 ★	8,643	79,117	85,128	795,298,394	10,052.18	9,342.38
1993	36,000 ★						

★ *estimated figures*

THE JOCKEY CLUB SCALE OF WEIGHTS FOR AGE

DISTANCE	AGE	JAN.	FEB.	MARCH	APRIL	MAY	JUNE	JULY	AUG.	SEPT.	OCT.	NOV.	DEC.
½ mile	2	x	x	x	x	x	x	x	105	108	111	114	114
	3	117	117	119	119	121	123	125	126	127	128	129	129
	4	130	130	130	130	130	130	130	130	130	130	130	130
	5&up	130	130	130	130	130	130	130	130	130	130	130	130
6 furlongs	2	x	x	x	x	x	x	x	102	105	108	111	111
	3	114	114	117	117	119	121	123	125	126	127	128	128
	4	129	129	130	130	130	130	130	130	130	130	130	130
	5&up	130	130	130	130	130	130	130	130	130	130	130	130
1 mile	2	x	x	x	x	x	x	x	x	96	99	102	102
	3	107	107	111	111	113	115	117	119	121	122	123	123
	4	127	127	128	128	127	126	126	126	126	126	126	126
	5&up	128	128	128	128	127	126	126	126	126	126	126	126
1¼ miles	2	x	x	x	x	x	x	x	x	x	x	x	x
	3	101	101	107	107	111	113	116	118	120	121	122	122
	4	125	125	127	127	127	126	126	126	126	126	126	126
	5&up	127	127	127	127	127	126	126	126	126	126	126	126
1½ miles	2	x	x	x	x	x	x	x	x	x	x	x	x
	3	98	98	104	104	198	111	114	117	119	121	122	122
	4	124	124	126	126	126	126	126	126	126	126	126	126
	5&up	126	126	126	126	126	126	126	126	126	126	126	126
2 miles	2	x	x	x	x	x	x	x	x	x	x	x	x
	3	96	96	102	102	106	109	112	114	117	119	120	120
	4	124	124	126	126	126	126	126	125	125	124	124	124
	5&up	124	124	126	126	126	126	126	125	125	124	124	124

A C K N O W L E D G E M E N T S

We would like to thank the following individuals for their help in creating this book: At The Jockey Club: Ogden Mills Phipps, Alan Marzelli, Daniel O'Connell, and Jim Peden. At International Creative Management: Amanda Urban, Sloan Harris, and Ann Taberski. At Bulfinch Press: Dan Farley, Patricia Burke Hansen, and Christina Eckerson.

For their help in locating and loaning pictures and illustrations, we would like to thank the following individuals and institutions: Katey Barret, Rayetta Burr, Benoit & Associates. Patty Lankford, *The Blood-Horse*. Mike Noonan, George S. Bolster Collection, Historical Society of Saratoga Springs. Ina Duncan, Churchill Downs/Kinetic Corporation. Dell Hancock. Jerry Cooke. Allen Reuben, Culver Pictures. Steve Stidham, Hollywood Park. Mrs. Walter M. Jeffords, Sarah Jeffords, Mae Alexander, Mrs. Walter M. Jeffords Collection. Cathy Schenk, Keeneland Library. Barbara D. Livingston. Norman Mauskopf. Beverly Carter, Paul Mellon Collection. Field Horne, Peter Hammell, National Museum of Racing and Hall of Fame. Bob Coglianese, New York Racing Association. Richard Stone Reeves. Jane Goldstein, Santa Anita Park. Mary Jane Kinney, *Sports Illustrated for Kids*. Tracy Gantz, *The Thoroughbred of California*. Mrs. John Hay Whitney, Nancy Little, Mrs. John Hay Whitney Collection.

THE EDITORS

AT LEFT
Greentree Training Stables, Saratoga. Painting by Vaughn Flannery. Courtesy Mrs. John Hay Whitney.

C A P T I O N S

AT LEFT
Photograph by Dell Hancock.

PAGE 180
Duettiste. Painting by Franklin B. Voss. Courtesy National Museum of Racing.

PAGE 188
Johnstown. Painting by Martin Stainforth.
Courtesy National Museum of Racing.

PAGE 190
Level Best. Painting by Martin Stainforth.
Courtesy National Museum of Racing.

PAGE 199
Devil Diver. Painting by Franklin B. Voss. Courtesy Mrs. John Hay Whitney.

PAGE 203
Count Fleet, John Longden up. Courtesy *The Blood-Horse*.

PAGE 206
Man o' War. Photograph by C. C. Cook Courtesy Keeneland-Cook.

PAGE 211
War Admiral. Painting by Richard Stone Reeves.

PAGE 213
Photograph by Norman Mauskopf.

PAGE 216
The Starting Gate, Saratoga. Painting by Vaughn Flannery.
Courtesy Mrs. John Hay Whitney.

PAGE 218
Photograph by Dell Hancock.

PAGE 220
Photograph by Dell Hancock.

ABOVE
Photograph by Norman Mauskopf.